ART IN THE REAL WORLD

WHAT IS COMPUTER ANIMATION?

JUDY THORPE

ROSEN PUBLISHING

Published in 2026 by The Rosen Publishing Group, Inc.
2544 Clinton Street, Buffalo, NY 14224

Portions of this work were originally authored by Hal Marcovitz and published as *Computer Animation*. All new material in this edition was authored by Judy Thorpe.

Designer: Rachel Rising
Editor: Jennifer Lombardo

Cataloging-in-Publication Data

Names: Thorpe, Judy.
Title: What is computer animation? / Judy Thorpe.
Description: Buffalo, NY : Rosen Publishing, 2026. | Series: Art in the real world | Includes glossary and index.
Identifiers: ISBN 9781499479218 (pbk.) | ISBN 9781499479225 (library bound) | ISBN 9781499479232 (ebook)
Subjects: LCSH: Computer animation--Juvenile literature. | Computer graphics Juvenile literature.
Classification: LCC TR897.72.S38 T486 2026 | DDC 777.7--dc23

Manufactured in the United States of America

CPSIA Compliance Information: Batch #CWRYA26. For further information, contact Rosen Publishing at 1-800-237-9932.

CONTENTS

FOREWORD

Art is a uniquely human endeavor. After all, no other kind of animal creates art, at least not without human intervention, and no other animal seems to appreciate art as a human would. Art is such an essential part of the human experience that art forms are numerous: paintings, drawings, sculptures, jewelry, dance, and much more. As civilizations developed, art forms became more plentiful and some more complex, such as architecture, films, and theater. In fact, art surrounds us to such a degree now and in such a variety of ways that sometimes we do not notice art for what it is.

To recognize the art that exists beyond museum walls, people may need to ask themselves what art is. It is certainly a difficult term to define. Most might say they know art when they see it. But do they? They might only recognize the most conventional forms of it.

Every brand of dictionary will include a slightly different interpretation of art's definition, but most would say art is an often-visual expression of thoughts, feelings, or emotions that is created through imagination and skill. Using this definition, we can understand that a more complete list of art forms should include graffiti, anime, fashion design, graphic design, and much more. Debates around these topics have been passionate and thought-provoking, with some people strongly arguing that they are indeed art and others just as strongly arguing that they are not.

This series asks readers to open their eyes and their minds to less conventional forms of art. As readers are introduced to the history of each art form, how it evolved, and what it looks like today, they will develop an appreciation for the ability and creativity needed to master each. They will learn how an artist may hone their talent for each art, whether they need to pursue a formal education, tips to get started in the field, the practical business side of it, and about some of the people who have "made it" as a successful artist in the art form.

Included in each text are quotes from experts, complete with citations to provide readers with sources for further research. Full-color photographs illustrate key points, helping readers visualize important concepts. Recommended books and websites also encourage young artists to explore related topics in more depth so that they can gain a greater appreciation for the art all around them in the real world.

Animation could be described as moving art.

INTRODUCTION

ANIMATION ADVANCEMENTS

Animated movies have been around since the early 1900s; the earliest known animated film is a three-minute short from 1906 called "Humorous Phases of Funny Faces." Early animations like this one consisted of simple drawings pieced together to form a sequence. Today, however, animators can transform a simple drawing or idea into a captivating, life-like finished product. Animations are now created across a wide spectrum of stylistic choices, using both new and old technology. Classic illustrated techniques can still be seen in films, TV shows, and video games, as well as advanced computer animations with realistic settings and characters. The work required to achieve either of these outcomes is a long process and includes the time and talents of many artists and engineers. Requiring both art and science to bring an animation to life, artists and engineers, along with a long list of creative and technologically skilled staff, work together to create a finished product.

The first animators practiced their craft through a process referred to as cel animation. This consisted of creating thousands of individual drawings on clear sheets, or cels (short for "celluloid," the material that the sheets were made of), that flowed together to form a sequence of scenes that in turn were strung together to create a time-lapsed story. Each cel drawing was photographed and subsequently fed quickly through a projector to show the movements of both the character and the background. This tedious process was the beginning of storytelling through film animation. Several well-known

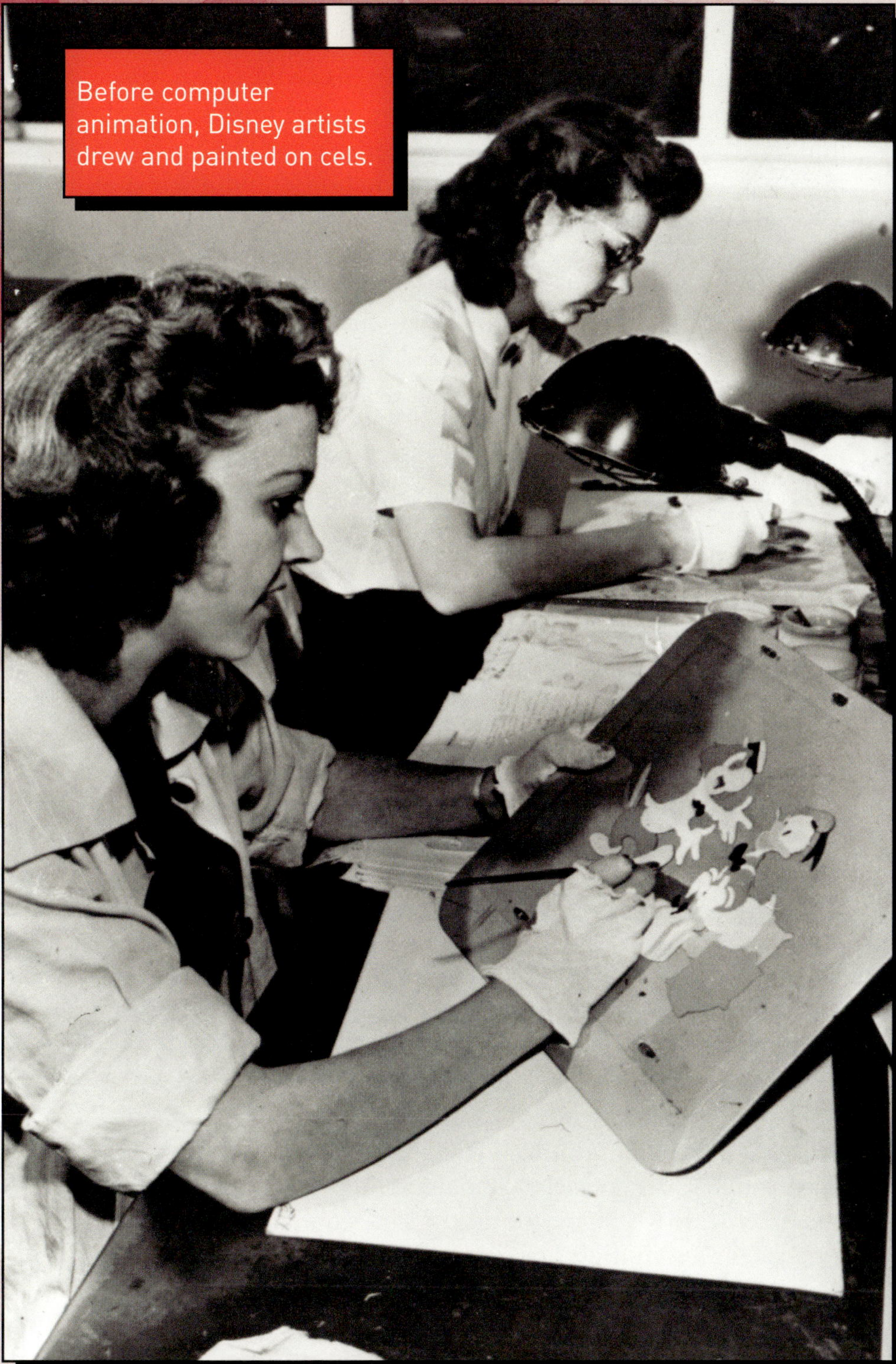

Before computer animation, Disney artists drew and painted on cels.

movies were created through this process. In 1937, Disney released the first fully animated movie, *Snow White and the Seven Dwarfs*. The cost for production of this film was $1.5 million. It quickly grossed $8 million after its release, revealing the possibilities of what film animation could achieve. Though this film was an unprecedented achievement at the time, it may seem outdated in comparison to today's computer animation. Even so, the technique of cel animation gives the film an artistic style that cannot be compared to the modern computer-generated form because they are so different, both in the way they are created and in how each finished product looks.

In the days of cel animation, the technology used for today's computer animation would have been unimaginable. These new techniques helped animators render three-dimensional forms and scenes, creating a more lifelike result. Computer-animated films are popular, though they remain distinguishable as cartoon-like animations. However, computer-generated images have opened up a new realm of possibilities, fusing computer-animated scenes and characters with real actors and sets. This fusion is used cohesively in many aspects of visual entertainment today, and advancements continue to progress and open more doors for improvements and new possibilities in computer animation technology.

The first full-length film generated entirely with computer animation techniques was released in 1995. This film, *Toy Story*, wowed audiences and critics and created a platform for many more animated films to come. Two of the largest animation companies, Pixar and Disney, created the masterpiece as a team. Steve Jobs, CEO of Pixar at the time, told *Fortune* magazine in September 1995, "If *Toy Story* is a modest hit—say $75 million at the box office—we'll both break even."[1] The film grossed approximately $361 million, a profit unimaginable before its release. After the film's extraordinary success, animators and executives at Disney and Pixar realized the magnitude of what computer animation could achieve. Multiple *Toy Story* sequels have been produced, and each new release has earned a profit significantly higher than the last.

Snow White was the first fully animated feature-length film in history. Animated short films, or shorts, were being made at that time, but not full movies.

The early pioneers of animation could not have imagined the advancements that computer animation has allowed for today and, with these advancements, the possibilities for both entertainment and everyday life that computer animation could and would provide.

Multiplane cameras took pictures of cels and gave them a 3D effect.

CHAPTER ONE

ANIMATION OVER TIME

Today, 3D computer animation tends to dominate the industry. It is considered the most advanced form of animation because, out of all the currently existing animation techniques, it has the ability to look the most lifelike. However, other animation styles are still used to create art.

Early forms of animation were created with little to no technology and were primarily executed by hand. These early practices provided a solid foundation for the advancement of animation. There were early attempts at motion pictures long before cel animation was able to capture images in motion. A technique called stop motion, which is still used in some works today, was one of the earliest animation methods. It involves taking a photo, moving the object in the frame slightly, taking another photo, and so on. The photos are eventually put together and shown so quickly that the objects appear to move on their own. This is similar to the effect a flipbook creates. Though basic in comparison to today's technology, early animation was incredibly groundbreaking in its time.

STARTING WITH CELS

The field of animation started with hand-drawn art. Some of the very first short films were done on chalkboards. Later, studios used cel animation to create animated films. The cels were transparent sheets of paper, onto which each illustration was drawn. For years, the sheets were made from cellulose. Today, however, cels are made from the synthetic substance acetate.

The *Steamboat Willie* animated short of 1928 was black and white but wowed audiences.

Creating a film through cel animation is an incredibly lengthy task. Even for the briefest features, thousands of cel drawings are created. Each scene for the film is illustrated onto a single cel. Scenes are often created in layers, with a bottom layer containing the background illustrations and several transparent sheets placed on top containing different stylistic elements and illustrations of the story. Most animators would shoot 1 cel per frame of film and then film the cartoon at a speed of 24 frames per second. Therefore, a 5-minute cartoon would require 7,200 cel drawings; for a 90-minute full-length feature film, artists produced nearly 130,000 cels.

In 1908, a French director, Émile Cohl, composed a brief animation titled *Fantasmagorie*. This piece is considered to be one of the first examples of an animated cartoon. The film, which is only a little more than one minute long, was produced using 700 simple black-and-white line drawings.

Cohl's work inspired many later animators, including Walt Disney. In 1911, American newspaper cartoonist Winsor McCay developed a two-minute animated film titled *Little Nemo*, which featured various storylines from the dreams of a young boy named Nemo. McCay drew each image for each frame of film himself. *Little Nemo* was a much more detailed animation in comparison to Cohl's *Fantasmagorie*. McCay began to understand the potential for animation and created several more successful short films throughout his lifetime.

One of the most notable early animators and the one who has been given the most credit for developing the craft of animation is Walt Disney. He produced the cartoon *Steamboat Willie* in 1928. The animated feature introduces the character Mickey Mouse as he navigates a steamboat over a river. It was an immediate hit among audiences. Animation historian Charles Solomon wrote, "Disney managed to book it into the Colony Theatre in New York for two weeks. *Steamboat Willie* premiered on November 18, 1928. The cartoon was a smash hit."[2] The film was produced in black and white, employing many techniques that print cartoonists had been using for years.

Steamboat Willie established Disney's studio, known by 1929 as Walt Disney Productions, as the preeminent animation studio of its day, and the studio has maintained that status for nearly a century, becoming one of the industry's top innovators. Mickey Mouse, first introduced in this short film, remains one of the world's best-known animated characters.

By the early 1930s, animators were employing simple colors in their features. Disney produced the first multicolor Mickey Mouse cartoon, *The Band Concert*, in 1935, followed by the first feature-length animated film, *Snow White and the Seven Dwarfs*, in 1937.

THE ANIMATION EXPLOSION

Through the efforts of Disney and many other creative people, cel animation became the standard for the industry, but other artists were also experimenting with alternative animation techniques, including stop-motion animation. When stop-motion animation uses clay figures, it is also sometimes called "claymation." As with cel animation, 24 frames are shot per second, which means the animator must move each object onscreen at least 24 times to produce 1 second of film. If there are two or three clay figures in the scene and each one is using its face, hands, and feet, there could be tens of thousands of manipulations required to produce only a few mintues of a film. Stop-motion animation proved to be a highly sophisticated form of art, and it continues to be used in films today. In the 1920s and 1930s, stop-motion animators were put to work by major Hollywood studios to produce images for some of the most popular movies of all time, including *King Kong* in 1933.

Following World War II, television exploded as an entertainment medium in the United States and elsewhere, and animators responded by providing programming for the new television networks. By the 1950s, animated cartoons such as *Crusader Rabbit*, *The Heckle and Jeckle Show*, and *The Woody Woodpecker Show*, as well as the claymation show *Gumby*, had arrived on television. While television became increasingly popular and more accessible, university computer laboratories were experimenting with different technological advancements that would eventually have a dramatic impact on the entertainment world.

Starting in the 1930s, at a time when audiences were awestruck by the animation of *Snow White and the Seven Dwarfs* and the stop-motion effects of *King Kong*, computers were first starting to come into use. One of the first computers, Harvard University's Mark I, was 50 feet (15.25 m) long, weighed 5 tons (4.5 mt), and took as long as 12 seconds to compute the simplest mathematical problem.

During World War II, computer technology made a great leap forward with the development of the University of Pennsylvania's Electronic Numerical Integrator and Computer (ENIAC), which was able to perform 100,000 calculations per second. ENIAC weighed 30 tons (27 mt) and required so much electricity that it occasionally dimmed the lights

Stop-motion involves moving objects so a photo series appears to show movement.

throughout the city of Philadelphia, Pennsylvania. ENIAC was developed with the help of funding from the United States military, which hoped to use the computer's data to pinpoint targets for artillery gunners. The war ended before the computer was finished. Nevertheless, the government liked what it had seen, and many computer-science research projects were funded by the military.

In 1951, a project at the Massachusetts Institute of Technology (MIT) known as Whirlwind produced a rudimentary flight simulator for the United States Navy. At the time, computers did not feature screens, but the MIT engineers were able to transfer the data to the screen of an oscilloscope, which could display simple graphics. Oscilloscopes had been used for many

BEHIND THE SCENES

Though many refinements have been made to the practice since the early 1900s, the look and feel of a stop-motion film is something that cannot be reproduced through average animation techniques. This is why it remains popular even today. One example is the movie *Coraline*, which was produced by the stop-motion animation studio Laika. *Coraline* was released in February 2009 and grossed more than $16 million in the United States during its first weekend alone. This film follows a girl named Coraline and her eerie adventures in an alternate world. The production team used props and characters modeled from clay for each sequence, which means that each moment was composed of thousands of different images. Since each clay prop was shifted around several different times, multiples of each small detail were constructed. The set even had a clothing designer who made hundreds of tiny costumes for each character. In 2018, a studio called Aardman Animations produced *Early Man*, an ambitious claymation movie that required 23 model makers, 273 clay puppets, and 3,000 interchangeable mouths to make the puppets' conversation and facial expressions look as natural as possible.

Aardman Animation Studios also created the beloved stop-motion characters Wallace and Gromit.

years to display impulses of electrical current produced by industrial equipment and similar devices. The image on the Whirlwind screen depicted the eastern coast of Massachusetts, while a symbol moved over the coast, simulating a flying aircraft. A major development in the project was the light pen stylus. When the light pen was pointed at the simulated aircraft, Whirlwind produced text on the screen that identified the plane as well as its speed and direction. This was the first example of being able to "click" to receive and move data on a computer screen.

COMPUTER SCIENTISTS SET THE STAGE

Scientists working at other university laboratories developed similar projects. In 1956, scientists at the University of Michigan were able to simulate the movements of military vehicles. In 1958, MIT scientists working under a United States Air Force contract developed a technique to print computer-generated pictures. Meanwhile, corporations started exploring computer imaging as well. In 1959, engineers at General Motors produced computer-generated drawings that were displayed on ordinary 35mm film. A year later, a scientist at Boeing Aircraft, William Fetter, coined the term "computer graphics" to describe the work he had been doing in designing the cockpits of airplanes.

By this time, computers were starting to employ screens to display text as well as graphics. In 1960, the Digital Equipment Company, one of the first computer manufacturers in the world, introduced the first computer equipped with a monitor—the Program Data Processor-1. It sold for $120,000. The Digital Equipment Company also equipped the device with a keyboard.

Meanwhile, other innovators developed techniques that would prove to be important to computerized filmmaking. In 1960, filmmaker John Whitney Sr. adapted a computer-driven device that armed an antiaircraft gun with a camera; using high-contrast photographic film, Whitney was able to produce abstract art. Whitney gained most of his knowledge of computers by taking them apart and putting them back

Often, CGI is done using a technique called "chroma keying," more commonly referred to as "green screen." In this technique, actors stand in front of a backdrop, or screen. Although the backdrop is frequently green, which is where the technique's nickname comes from, it can be any color. The actors film their scenes, and the background is added later. Characters also sometimes wear special green suits that allow animators to replace them later with CGI effects. Chroma keying is typically done to make special effects easier, safer, or more cost effective. For example, in the movie *Jurassic World*, actor Chris Pratt filmed many of his scenes alongside people in crude dinosaur costumes, all of whom were in front of a green screen. The people in costumes helped Pratt know where to look when he was acting. Later, the background was filled in and the humans in costumes were replaced with CGI dinosaurs. Earlier Jurassic Park movies used animatronic dinosaurs, which were large, moving models. *Jurassic World: Dominion*, the third movie in the trilogy, also featured animatronics in some scenes because it was easier for the actors to interact with them. However, CGI made it possible to get realistic shots of dinosaurs running and attacking, so it was still used in many parts of the movie.

The first film to employ CGI was *Westworld*, which was released in 1973. *Westworld* tells the story of a futuristic amusement park where guests can play the parts of Wild West characters. Some of the characters in this film are portrayed as robots. *Westworld* features scenes from the robots' points of view. To show the audience what the robot is seeing, the image was scrambled by the computer, which resulted in a pixilated version of the actual scene.

Although many movies today use CGI in various ways to create realistic effects, the early technology was not sophisticated. In the 1970s and 1980s, CGI looked clunky and boxy. Movies where it was used extensively tend to look silly and dated today. One example is the 1984 movie *The Last Starfighter*. It used CGI for the spaceships, and to a viewer in 2025, that fact is instantly clear. In contrast, the ship from 2009's *District 9* appears hyper-realistic. In only two decades, computer animation had advanced by leaps and bounds.

In 1977, *Star Wars* made cinematic history. The story of intergalactic rebels fighting against an evil empire generated a worldwide audience that was suddenly hungry for science-fiction adventures. By no means was *Star Wars* an animated film; it featured actors, life-sized props and sets, and live-action filming. The director, George Lucas, made wide use of miniatures and other well-established special-effects techniques.

However, Lucas did use CGI in some parts of the movie. For example, when the rebels discuss how to destroy the Death Star, they look at plans of the ship's layout. Those plans were CGI. The technology was not yet advanced enough to use it for more things. However, when the movies were remastered and re-released in the late 1990s, many more CGI effects were added. For instance, some of the aliens in the cantina, which had originally been people in costumes, were replaced with CGI characters. There is some debate among Star Wars fans about whether these CGI additions made the movies better or worse.

WORKING TOGETHER

In 1975, Lucas established his own special-effects company to develop the CGI for his own films as well as other studios willing to pay for his services. He named the company Industrial Light and Magic. As Lucas worked on his sequel to *Star Wars,* titled *The Empire Strikes Back*, he created a new division of Industrial Light and Magic. This division would concentrate solely on developing techniques and equipment that filmmakers could use to produce CGI effects. The division, which he called the Graphics Group, developed some truly advanced research.

In 1986, the Graphics Group struck out on its own as an independent company. The employees named the company Pixar, which is the name they gave one of the computers they used to create CGI. The only investor Lucas could find for the new company was Steve Jobs, one of the founders of Apple Computers.

The employees at Pixar wanted to create animated movies, but they knew the technology was not ready yet; any movie made in the 1980s with CGI was going to look silly to audiences. While experts worked on improving the technique, Pixar stayed afloat by developing the computers that ran the CGI programs. One of the company's earliest customers turned out to be the Disney studio, which employed Pixar's hardware as well as Pixar's special company software to produce images for its animated films. Disney was the first studio to use a computer to produce the images that cel artists had been doing for years. In 1990, Disney produced *The Rescuers Down Under.* It was the first animated film to use this automated process. Disney combined cel animation with digital animation by scanning the artists' drawings of the characters and backgrounds into the computer. They were then inked and colored on the computer by digital artists, the way many artists today use a tablet to create drawings. The Pixar computer software could then be used to add special effects, such as changing virtual camera angles.

In 1991, Steve Jobs bought Pixar; instead of being just a shareholder, or even the majority shareholder, he was now the owner. That same year, the Disney film *Beauty and the Beast* included sequences produced by Pixar's computers. Most of the film was produced through cel animtion, but the backgrounds in the ballroom sequence—in which Belle first dances with the Beast—were rendered by computer animation. If the ballroom scene had been hand-painted by artists, it would have been a flat, two-dimensional rendering, and the characters would simply have danced across a static background. By using a computer, the filmmakers were able to add a three-dimensional perspective to the background, changing the viewpoint of the scenery as the two characters danced through it. As *Beauty and the Beast* producer Don Hahn recalled,

> *The ballroom sequence is the bonding moment of the film when the two main characters finally get together. For us*

Beauty and the Beast blended elements of both cel animation and computer animation.

filmmakers, the computer offered us a way to get heightened emotions on the screen and more dramatic effects than we could have gotten conventionally. It allowed us to move the camera around and take a look at the room instead of just looking at a flat piece of artwork. Technology as a whole is an extension of our fingers, hands, and minds. Computer graphics let us go beyond what we can currently achieve with pencil and paper or paint and a brush.[4]

The dazzling computer animation included in the film helped *Beauty and the Beast* win an Academy Award (also known as an Oscar) nomination for Best

Pixar Animation Studios' *Toy Story* was so popular that it had multiple sequels and a spin-off movie, *Lightyear*.

Picture in 1992—making it the first animated film ever to receive an Oscar nomination in that category.

A year later, the Disney film *Aladdin* made even more use of computer animation. In the film, Pixar computers created the animated sequences inside the Cave of Wonders and also produced every image of the magic carpet that is featured in the film. It was the first time a complete character in a feature film was animated by the computer.

After the success of *Beauty and the Beast* and *Aladdin*, it became clear to executives at Pixar and Disney that a full-length feature film could be produced entirely through computer animation. In 1995, Pixar and Disney partnered to produce *Toy Story*. The story presents the adventures of toys that come to life. The film features the voices of Tom Hanks as Woody, the toy cowboy, and Tim Allen as Buzz Lightyear, the toy space ranger.

After Hanks and Allen read the dialogue in a recording studio, some 300 technicians spent a total of 800,000 hours behind their computer screens, fashioning the artwork for the 81-minute movie. It took up to 15 hours of work to produce each frame of film. The work paid off; in *Toy Story*, audiences saw a style of animation unfold on the screen that they had never seen before. That film's success helped launch an entirely new kind of feature-length filmmaking. Since then, *Toy Story* has become so wildly popular that multiple sequels have been made. *Toy Story* 5 is set to release in 2026.

LEADERS IN COMPUTER ANIMATION

In 2006, Disney agreed to buy Pixar for more than $7 billion—showing how important and profitable the computer animation studio had become in the industry. Since then, Disney and Pixar have gone on to produce some of the most profitable movies of all time. Though the companies sometimes function as separate entities, more so Disney than Pixar, the Disney-Pixar collaboration is to thank for most of the top animated movies today, including *Finding Dory*.

REMADE WITH CGI

A new *Beauty and the Beast* film was released in March 2017. The recreation of the film featured the same storyline, with an updated cast of computer-generated characters. Unlike the first film, where just the ballroom scene was produced through the computer, almost all the scenes in the remake included some sort of computer-generated material. Many of the characters in the remake were almost entirely computer-generated, with the exception of a few, including the main character, Belle, played by Emma Watson. The Beast, however, was a mix between motion-capture technology and computer-generated material. The character was voiced and played by actor Dan Stevens, who acted out several scenes, which were then animated over on the computer to portray the Beast. Since a real person played the part of Belle, making the Beast look realistically comparable was crucial to making this film a success. The divide between the live-action elements with the animated ones in this film needed to be seamless, allowing those "heightened emotions" to take place without questioning the authenticity of the characters.

The live-action *Beauty and the Beast* was a success, making over $1 billion.

Pixar is one of the most consistently successful and acclaimed animation studios, blending strong artwork and powerful storytelling.

The Minions were a creation of DreamWorks Animation, which is owned by Universal Studios. They are featured at Universal Studios theme parks too.

Finding Dory was released in June 2016 and had the highest-grossing animated movie debut in U.S. history. Other popular titles created by Disney-Pixar include *Inside Out*, *Up*, *Cars*, and *Wall-E*. Disney, on the other hand, has independently created successful computer-animated movies such as *Zootopia*, *Frozen*, *Big Hero 6*, and *Moana*.

Today, Pixar faces competition from more than a dozen computer animation companies, some of which are underwritten by Hollywood's most important studios. One of Pixar's main competitors is the computer animation division of DreamWorks. The studio, founded by director Steven Spielberg, has produced movies such as *Trolls*, *Shrek*, and *Kung Fu Panda*. DreamWorks remains one of the most profitable animation companies, though it has had fewer top box office hits than Disney and Pixar.

Another studio with several notable computer-animated films is Universal Pictures. It was founded in 1912 and has produced many highly rated films, both animated and live action. The studio's most notable computer-animated films include *Despicable Me*, *Despicable Me 2*, *Minions*, and *The Secret Life of Pets*.

Other companies that provide CGI effects are also in high demand. Since animation has spanned not only to 3D graphics in film, but also to animation in live-action movies, studios like Industrial Light and Magic are still a huge part of the animation industry. Industrial Light and Magic has provided special effects for many top films such as those in the Star Wars, Jurassic Park, and Pirates of the Caribbean film franchises. It is now overseen by Disney because Disney purchased its parent company, Lucasfilm, in 2012. Since then, Disney has owned the rights not only to Industrial Light and Magic, but also to the Star Wars stories and characters.

As time goes on, more and more advancements are made in the field of computer animation. This has broadened what animators are able to do. The goal is not always to make the most realistic-looking things. Like other forms of art, animation comes in different styles. Blending computer animation with traditional 2D animation, claymation, and other styles allows animators flexibility when creating projects.

One style that is gaining popularity is a mix of 2D and 3D animation. Movies such as *Spider-Man: Into the Spider-Verse* and TV shows such as *Arcane* have received praise from viewers for their mix of styles. *Into the Spider-Verse* animates characters differently within the same scene, which helps differentiate them from each other and drive home the idea that they all come from different universes. *Arcane* uses a technique in which 2D animation is drawn onto a 3D scaffolding. This means that while the characters' faces and outfits have a 2D drawing style, they move like a 3D character. Disney also used a mix of animation styles for *Wish*, the movie that marked the company's 100th anniversary. For this film, animators used 3D characters in front of 2D painted backgrounds, blending the new style of movies such as *Frozen* and *Encanto* with the old style that movies such as *Sleeping Beauty* were known for.

Spider-Man: Across the Spider-Verse was a 2023 film produced by Columbia Pictures and Sony Pictures Animation.

CHAPTER TWO

A SHORT HISTORY OF GAMES

People quickly realized that computers had possibilities beyond animating movies. One of the biggest alternatives to film animation is animation in video games. Progress in animation allowed artists and programmers to create animated games that could be altered and directed according to the moves and decisions of the player. What is now an industry that brings in billions of dollars a year started out just as film animation did—a simple concept that evolved into a more advanced product.

Today, there are video games where the characters on-screen look and move like real people, almost indistinguishable as animation. Technology has advanced far enough that virtual reality headsets are available that essentially block those wearing them from the outside world, allowing users to interact and play along solely with the alternate world in front of them. Science journalist Keith Ferrell stated, "Graphics, sound, motion: All must come together to create a believable illusion. The goal, some feel, is interactive fiction as striking in image and sound as motion pictures."[5] All of these believable illusions were made possible by the experiments and accomplishments of various early game designers and animation pioneers.

EARLY GAME ANIMATION

One of the earliest games that sparked the gaming industry was created in 1961 by a group of students at MIT.

They used the school's new Program Data Processor-1 (PDP-1) computer to develop a game they called *Spacewar!* The game featured the simplest of graphics—basically points of light on the screen—but players could maneuver a spaceship around a star while battling enemy ships. The PDP-1's manufacturer, the Digital Equipment Company, eventually received permission from the students to distribute the game along with the PDP-1. Therefore, anybody who had access to a PDP-1 could play *Spacewar!* Of course, since a PDP-1 computer cost \$120,000, the game was played mostly in university laboratories, corporate computer departments, military installations, and other institutions that could afford expensive computer equipment. As such, it was not available in the consumer market. Still, during the 1960s, engineers and software designers continued to experiment with manipulating images on computer screens, knowing that eventually electronic games could be fashioned for home players.

Later, in 1966, a man by the name of Ralph Baer began creating what would be known as the first video game console—the Magnavox Odyssey. The gaming system was released in 1972. This console, which connected to a television set, featured 12 different games. All were variations of light movement on the screen and required different plastic overlays to be placed on the television screen for the view of the games to function properly. Games included sports such as hockey and football, as well as casino games such as roulette. Although it was the first at-home console that worked with a television, since it was marketed at \$100 and could only be used with a Magnavox television set, it was unattainable by most consumers.

AN ICONIC COMPUTER GAME

A frequent gamer, Nolan Bushnell, became inspired by the aspects of *Spacewar!* and the opportunities that both computer-based and television-based games could hold. He became interested in game development when he was a college student, often playing *Spacewar!* on the computers at the University of Utah, where he received an engineering degree in 1968.

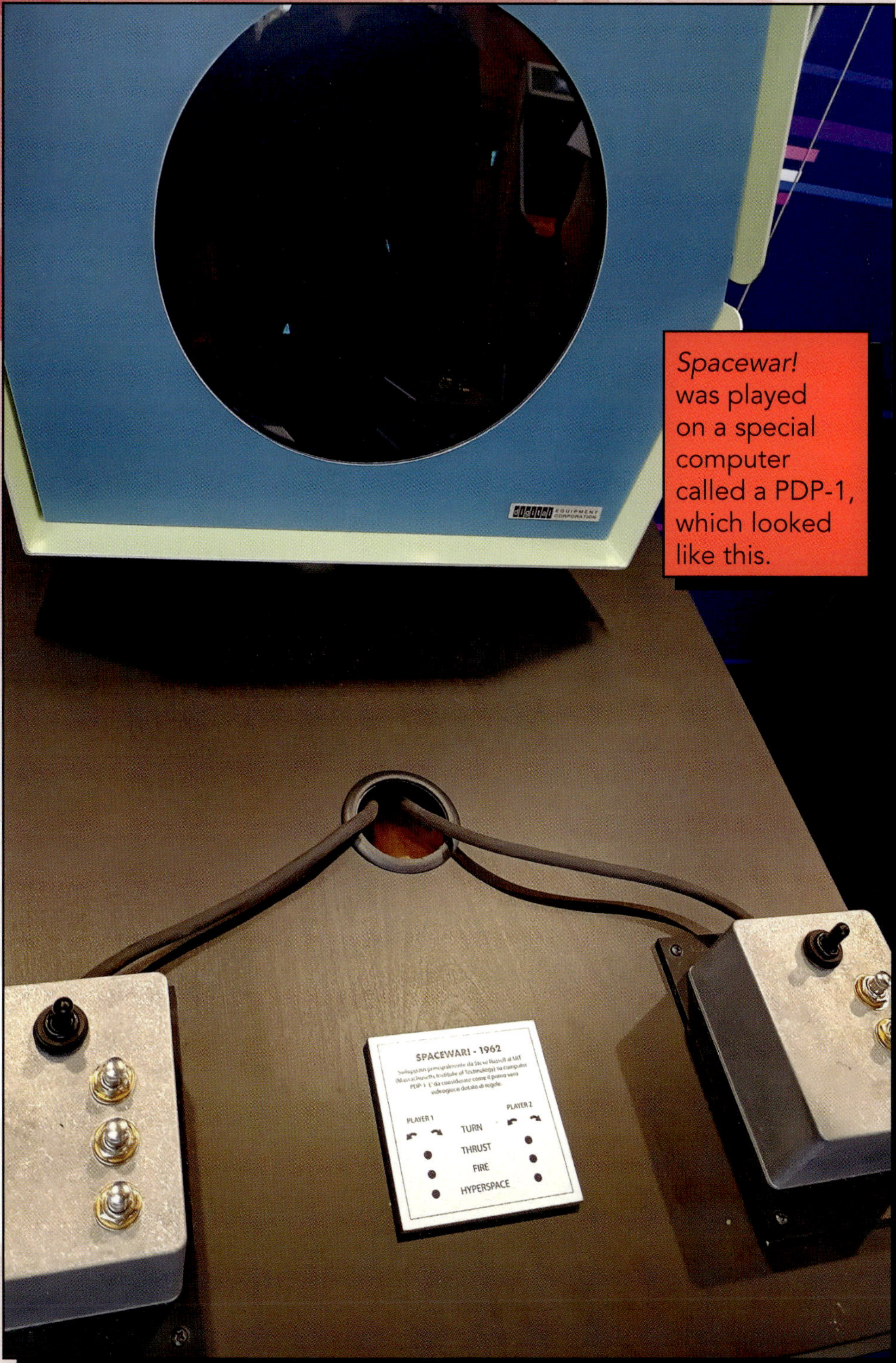

Spacewar! was played on a special computer called a PDP-1, which looked like this.

Bushnell went on to become one of the most notable pioneers in the development of video games. He became one of the founders of the electronic game industry when he developed *Pong* and later established Atari.

After graduating in 1968, Bushnell and his friend Ted Dabney adapted *Spacewar!* to play on an ordinary black-and-white television set and renamed the game *Computer Space*. They developed a hardware console that hooked to the television. The console—a rudimentary computer—could do nothing more than play the game on the television. They formed a company named Syzygy to sell the game, but they were able to sell just a few models. Players found the instructions too difficult, and Syzygy was soon out of business.

Bushnell and Dabney learned a valuable lesson from the failure of *Computer Space*, and they resolved to develop a new game that would be more user-friendly. Bushnell recalled, "To be successful, I had to come up with a game people already knew how to play."[6] They each contributed $250 and started a new company, which they named Atari, which is the word for a maneuver in the Japanese board game Igo. The first game they developed was an electronic version of ping-pong, which they called *Pong*.

Instead of building new consoles for home sales, Bushnell and Dabney released *Pong* as an arcade game. They envisioned it standing next to pinball machines in bars, soda shops, and bowling alleys.

A *Pong* machine was nothing more than a blank screen that featured a white dot smacked back and forth by the players, who used knobs to control the two virtual paddles. There were even sound effects; when a player hit the "ball," the machine emitted a definitive "plink."

In 1972, the first *Pong* game was installed in a bar named Andy Capp's in San Jose, California. Bushnell and Dabney set up the *Pong* console next to a pinball machine. There was one line of instruction printed alongside the screen: "Avoid missing ball for high score."[7] By the second day, the machine had broken from overuse. Bushnell and Dabney returned to fix it. At the end of the first week, the *Pong* machine earned the inventors

Pong was a simple two-dimensional video game, but many found it addictive to play.

a bright red hat to avoid animation complications. This character was later called Mario.

To name the game, Miyamoto proposed to use the word Kong in the title because it suggested the image of an ape. He also flipped through a Japanese-English dictionary and found the word "donkey," which in Japanese means "stupid" or "goofy." Therefore, he had the name for the game: *Donkey Kong*. After production was completed, the game was shipped to the United States for distribution. Marketing teams were given the task of translating the instructions and game text to English, and with that, developing English names for the characters. The ape would still be named Donkey Kong. The princess, Pauline, was named after the wife of a Nintendo employee in the United States, and the main character of the game, Mario, was named after the company's disgruntled warehouse owner.

Donkey Kong proved to be enormously successful. The first 2,000 arcade machines sold quickly, and another 60,000 were soon shipped from Japan. In its first 2 years, *Donkey Kong* earned Nintendo sales of more than $100 million. Soon after the game arrived in the United States, Nintendo licensed the title to Coleco, an American company, to produce a home version. In fact, many of the most popular games were being produced for home consoles to be played on televisions as well as personal computers, which were becoming more of a presence in American homes. Nintendo and the other game manufacturers found they could license the games to software companies, which adapted the titles so they could be played on home computers.

Today, Nintendo remains one of the leading video game companies. In 1990, it created the Game Boy. This gaming system was able to function alone, without the need for a television or computer. The portable console was created with a tiny screen and movement buttons below. A game cartridge was inserted into the back of the handheld console. This was a huge step in the gaming industry. In 1998, an updated version of the console was released that featured colored animation for the games. Today, much

Donkey Kong used 8-bit animation. Some recent video games still use this iconic style.

BETTER GRAPHICS

Several other consoles have dominated the world of gaming for years. In 2001, Microsoft released the Xbox, a new gaming console that offered high-resolution images and a cleaner, more seamless way of playing. A year later, Xbox Live was released, allowing people to connect with other users through the internet and play with them interactively through the gaming console. A new game was released with the Xbox that was specific to its console. The game *Halo* is a first-person shooter game where the player must accomplish missions and unlock different secrets as they go. The graphics of this game were a big step for CGI. Though they were still noticeably animated, the characters represented real people in a way that felt similar to live action.

The *Tomb Raider* series illustrates how animation style has changed since the 1990s.

more advanced versions of these products are available. The Nintendo DS, first released in 2005, offered a flip-phone style with two screens—one for viewing the game and the other to make movements and choose options. A newer model, the Nintendo 3DS, features 3D graphics and allows the player to maneuver through the game, playing the characters seamlessly through the portable console. In 2016, the Nintendo Switch came out, named for the fact that players can switch between using it as a handheld console and using the controllers to play the games on their TV.

FROM MOVIES TO GAMES AND BACK AGAIN

George Lucas, the producer of the Star Wars movies, realized that the characters and scenarios from the films could be adapted into games. He established LucasArts, a division of his entertainment company devoted to producing games. Games such as X-*Wing*, *Rebel Assault*, and *Dark Forces* were adapted from Star Wars scenarios. Lucas also produced the films in the Indiana Jones series. Two games featuring the heroic archaeologist Indiana Jones were developed.

By the 1990s, game designers were able to provide far more graphics, speed, color, and action because of the advancements in computer technology—particularly the microprocessor, which is the tiny device in the computer that relays the user's commands to the computer, instructing the machine on what to do. Home computers had become sophisticated and were able to accept a higher degree of graphics and animation. In 1996, hardware manufacturers added a microprocessor to home machines that enabled the monitors to display graphics in three dimensions. Now players could control animated characters—seeing them from all sides and changing their viewpoints, directions, and paths through the games.

One game that shows the sophistication in animation techniques during this period debuted in 1996. The game, titled *Tomb Raider*, featured an animated main character—Lara Croft. The game designers of *Tomb Raider* wanted to make the characters and scenes seem as realistic as possible, blurring the lines between real life

BALDUR'S GATE

Baldur's Gate 3 is a video game that was released in 2023. It can be played on several different platforms, including PC (personal computer), PlayStation, and Xbox. The game has been widely praised for its graphics. The texture of things such as clothing, hair, and skin are highly detailed, and updates made after the game's release included fog and clouds that look and move realistically. Still photos of the characters look nearly indistinguishable from real people, and their movements in the game are fairly smooth, although moving images make it clearer that the characters are animated.

Although *Baldur's Gate 3* was meticulously and lovingly animated by a team that took their jobs very seriously, a computer's graphics card can make or break the gameplay experience. No matter how well the animators did their job, a poor graphics card can prevent a player from seeing all the details. As one reviewer put it, "It feels like putting on a clearer pair of glasses to see everything with."[1] Gamers who want to get the best experience should research which graphics cards are recommended for the setup they have.

1. Shannon Liao, "Revisiting Baldur's Gate 3 with a Way Better Graphics Card Changed Everything—Or Did It?," Inverse, February 18, 2025. https://www.inverse.com/gaming/baldurs-gate-3-nvidia-gtx-5090-revisiting.

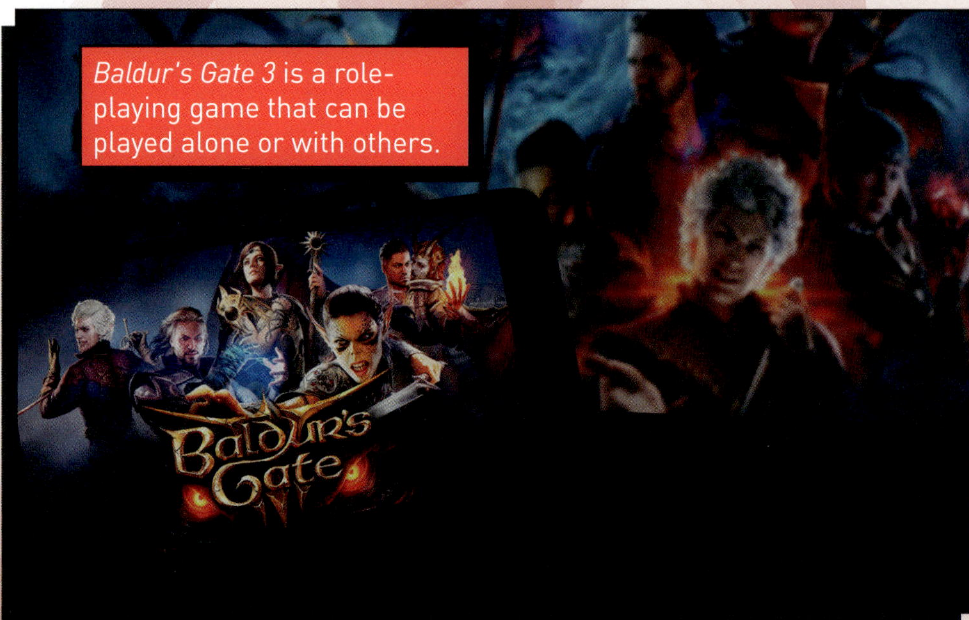

Baldur's Gate 3 is a role-playing game that can be played alone or with others.

The Witcher books inspired a video game series and a TV series.

and animation. However, they were working with technology that was not yet far enough along for them to do that. While the results were beyond anything that had been seen at the time, today the graphics look outdated.

The purpose of the game was to retrieve ancient artifacts and battle villains along the way. In 2001, the game was adapted into a live-action movie starring Angelina Jolie as Lara Croft. This was one of the first examples of a video game being converted into a film.

Today, it is very common to see movies and TV shows based on video games. Some examples include:

- *The Last of Us*
- *Minecraft*
- *Resident Evil*
- *Fallout*
- *Sonic the Hedgehog*
- *Uncharted*
- *Halo*
- *Five Nights at Freddy's*
- *The Witcher*

It is less common to see video games based on TV shows and movies, but it is not unheard of. One example is a *Stranger Things* video game. It was created by Netflix to go along with that show. Netflix games are included for free to Netflix subscribers. Other examples include *Ghostbusters*, *Scott Pilgrim vs. the World*, and *X-Men Origins: Wolverine*.

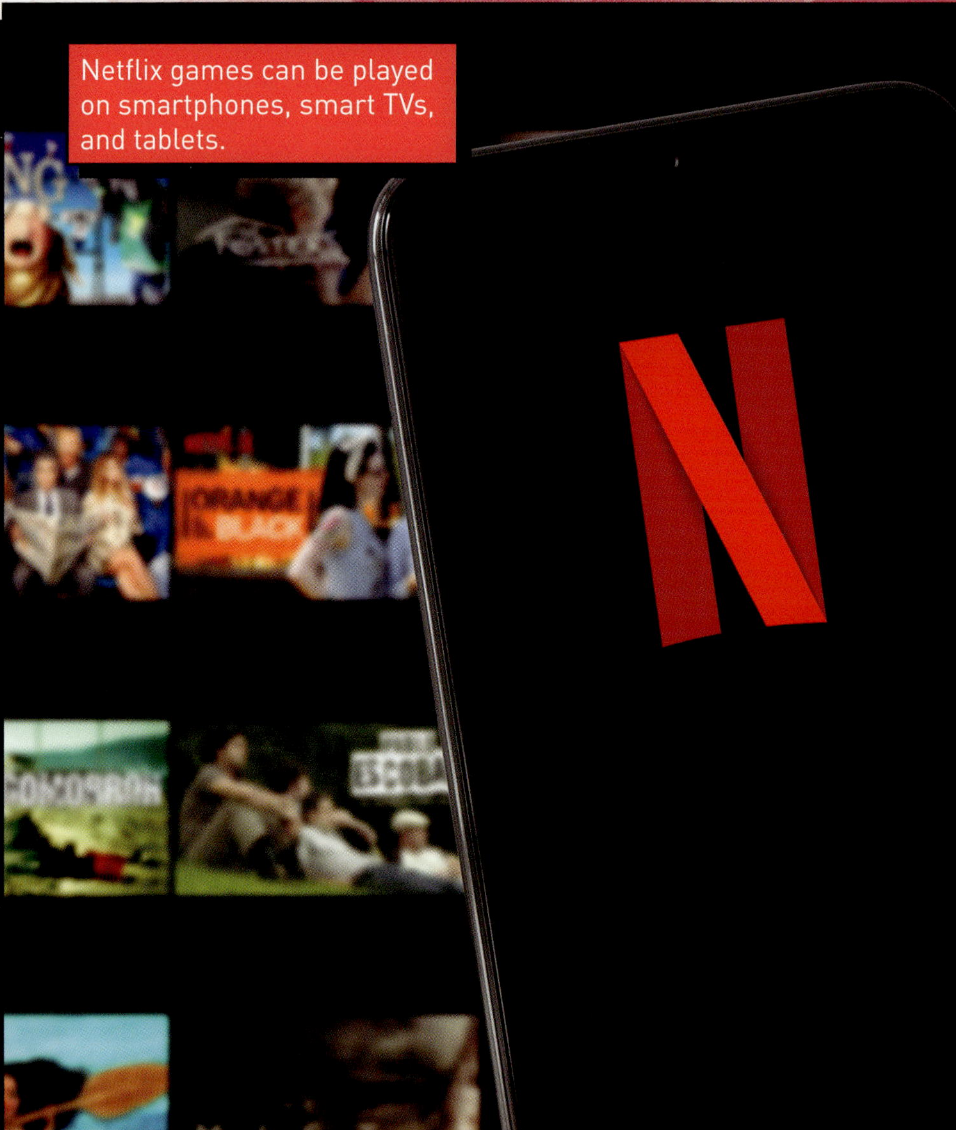

Netflix games can be played on smartphones, smart TVs, and tablets.

CHAPTER THREE

A WORK IN PROGRESS

Even with the help of advanced computers, it takes a lot of work to create an animated movie. Each character requires a specific range of movements and a complex means of manipulating their face and body to match those movements flawlessly. This keeps the viewer from being distracted and allows them to enjoy the experience in front of them—whether the medium is film, television, or a video game.

When animators working on the film *Monsters, Inc.*, and later, on its prequel, *Monsters University*, designed the big blue monster named Sulley, they found it necessary to employ a unique computer program that enabled them to move each strand of Sulley's fur—all 2.3 million of them. Creating this computer program required the talents of several software engineers. Once the program was in place, animators were able to alter each aspect of the character, allowing him to move in a way that looked natural. In the case of *Monsters, Inc.*, this included allowing each strand of Sulley's fur to shift according to his physical movements.

Most animators working professionally today are graduates of art schools rather than computer science programs. Meanwhile, the software used to make these animations possible comes from mathematical formulas known as algorithms. Though animators are the people who create and manipulate the art that makes animation possible, software engineers play a big part in its creation. Frequently, specific software needs to be written to achieve the specific goals of a project, and animators and software engineers must work

In the 2012 film *Brave*, Merida's hair was animated to move realistically.

closely together to create a successful animation. At Pixar, former chief creative officer John Lasseter said the company had invested heavily in technology, while keeping in mind that the artists are the ones who provide Pixar with its cinematic vision. As Lasseter explained, "Here, the art challenges the technology and the technology inspires the art."[8] Without the technological advances that have occurred throughout the history of animation, the process that makes it so successful today would not exist.

PLANNING AHEAD

When it comes to animating on the computer, artists find themselves involved early in the process. All films—whether they are live-action, rendered on the computer, or produced through cel art—begin with a concept, a script, and then a storyboard. Concepts and then scripts are typically provided by writers or the people who conceive the story. Script writers plot out the action and compose the dialogue. After the initial concept is fleshed out, storyboarding is the next step. Drawn by artists, storyboards provide the initial visualization for how the films will look. This is a crucial part in mapping out each step for the filmmakers so that when they begin creating the film, they have a concrete vision to bring to life.

Storyboards have been used in moviemaking for decades—and not just in animated films. Essentially, an artist is called on to draw the movie, scene by scene, on large poster boards. Storyboards are often rather detailed, as their purpose is to give the director an idea of how each scene should be photographed. Working from a storyboard, a director can plot placement of cameras and sound equipment, choose the lenses for the cameras, plan how to light the scene, and decide where to stage the actors. In live-action filmmaking, storyboarding serves as a general outline. Since directors are able to see each scene acted out in real time, actors are able to move and shift to create a more accurate depiction of the initial ideas for that particular scene.

In computer animation, animators pay strict adherence to what the storyboard tells them to do. The storyboard is very detailed because it is used to guide the animators in how to render the characters in each scene. In a film that is animated by the computer, one scene must end where the next one begins. Most animated films employ dozens or often hundreds of artists, all developing different scenes at the same time. Artists may take months to animate the scenes they have been assigned.

If an artist does not strictly follow the storyboard, a choppy scene-to-scene transition may result. This does not mean that no changes can be made to the movie after the storyboard phase; sometimes scenes get cut or changed when they are partially or even fully animated, just as some scenes from live-action movies get cut after they are filmed. However, the storyboard is more than just a suggestion; it is an important guideline in the moviemaking process, whether that movie is animated or not. Patrick Kriwanek, an animation professor at the University of California, Berkeley, explained the process:

A storyboard includes sketches of each scene of a narrative.

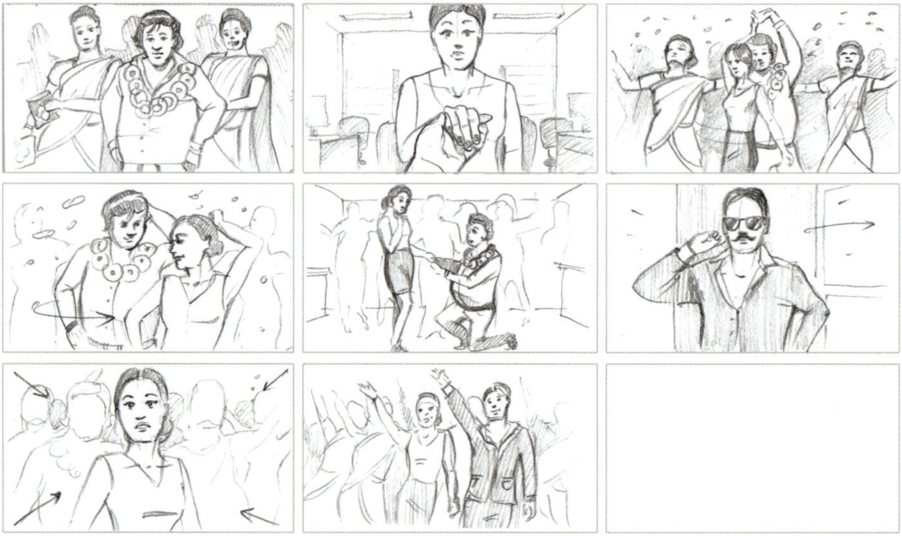

In film, no shot exists alone; it is a sister to the incoming shot, and must flow into the next shot. It exists as part of a full-motion continuum, and it has to be pre-visualized in that way … that is why the boards for Finding Nemo *or* Toy Story *look exactly like the boards for* Indiana Jones, *because those boards were created by filmmakers, thinking and visualizing the shots in continuity, in service of the greater flow …The greatest animated films of our time are great because they "feel" like a real movie, they have been constructed by filmmakers using the same guidelines we use to create powerful live-action narratives.*[9]

CHARACTER DESIGN

Following the storyboarding phase, the process moves into the computer. The first step in bringing a computer-animated scene to life is known as modeling. The artists who work in this phase of production are known as modelers. Typically, modelers have backgrounds in sculpture or industrial design.

A model is any three-dimensional object—most often a character—that will appear in the scene. Sometimes modeling is done by fashioning a sculpture, known as a maquette, of the character that will later be scanned into the computer. If they choose not to work from maquettes, modelers can work right on the computer, composing a character using one of two methods: polygon modeling or spline modeling.

Polygon modeling is based on a form of industrial design that was developed in 1949 by the architect R. Buckminster Fuller, who used it to design the geodesic dome. A geodesic dome is a sphere constructed by linking together the sides of triangles or similar geometric shapes, known as polygons, and angling them each slightly so they fit together to form a sphere. Modelers can fashion shapes as complicated as Sulley by building the characters through polygon construction on their computers. Generally, the first step includes scanning a sketch of the character into the computer. Next, the modeler selects points on the image that provide a general outline of the character. The

Rocket Raccoon and Baby Groot models, or maquettes, helped animate the characters in the Marvel film *Guardians of the Galaxy*.

computer software will then add a series of lines connecting the points. It is similar to making a sculpture out of papier-mâché; in that medium, the artist first constructs a wire skeleton on which the papier-mâché will be applied. Once a computer-animated character's skeleton has been created, the modeler can use the software to fill in the gaps with polygons. For highly detailed work that will show many curves, crevices, corners, wrinkles, bumps, hairs, and other assorted features, the polygons need to be tiny and packed closely together. This tedious process requires sophisticated computer software as well as the work of many talented modelers.

The other method of creating a character on the computer is known as splining. Campers are familiar with splines because they use them as the ribs to support domed tents. Campers first set up the splines, creating a skeleton, then stretch the tent fabric over them. As in polygon modeling, a spline modeler will first scan the drawing and then select the reference points to create the outline and skeleton of the character. Instead of filling in the gaps with polygons, the modeler will use splines. Splining can be accomplished with less-powerful computers than those required to produce a model with polygons, but polygons provide a more intricately detailed model. The major animation studios, with multimillion-dollar budgets at their disposal and hundreds of modelers and animators on staff, generally prefer to work with the polygon method.

RIGGING

Whether the artist works with splines or polygons, the modeler has now created a character in two dimensions. To create a three-dimensional character, other viewpoints of the character must be modeled. For a simple shape, modelers can compose three-dimensional viewpoints by working with additional sketches of the same object. For example, a modeler can compose a three-dimensional image of a bouncing ball by using sketches. This technique may not work for more complex objects or characters; in those cases, the modelers must make use of maquettes. In the large animation studios, modelers will use clay to fashion maquettes of the characters. Maquettes are generally about 14 inches (35.5 cm) tall.

The maquettes do not have to be very intricate. Later, the details of the characters' faces and bodies can be fine-tuned on the computer. The purpose of the maquette is to provide the reference points for the computer that the modeler can use to fill in with polygons or splines. After the maquette is fashioned, the modeler will typically draw a grid of black lines across its surface. Each place on the maquette where the lines of the grid intersect creates a reference point. The modeler can then use a handheld scanning device to transmit the reference points to the computer.

The computer now has in its memory every conceivable viewpoint of the figure. Whenever a viewpoint is called up on the computer monitor, the reference points are filled in with polygons or splines. At this point, the modeler may work for weeks or months refining the images by filling in intricate details, colors, and other features.

The character is now ready for the next step, which is known as rigging. Using the computer, the artist known as the rigger finds places on the character where the image can be manipulated to show motion. Most living things move their body at the joints in their arms, legs, neck, back, feet, hands, and other limbs. Likewise, on the computer, the rigger selects places on the character's body that will serve as joints. To select the joints, the rigger will superimpose a temporary skeleton over the image of the character. When the film is shown in theaters, the audience will never see the skeleton—it will be erased long before the graphics are transferred to film—but it is vital as a tool for showing the animators where the character can bend a leg, crook a finger, or form words with his or her mouth.

According to Peter Weishar, a professor and computer animation expert, rigging is one of the most important parts of animation because it governs how the character moves. As Weishar explains, how the animator designs the movements of the character is often the most vital task in convincing the audience of the authenticity of the character: "Even if the character is something as unlikely as a talking giant sloth walking

Animation software today makes the process of animating much easier than in the early days of cels and hand-painting.

MOVING MOUTHS

One of the most important things to "rig" in an animation are the facial expressions of a character—more specifically, a character's mouth and lips. This job is particularly important because the lips must move in sync with the dialogue spoken in the sound studio by the actor providing the voice for the character.

To properly rig the lips, the rigger must understand how sounds are formed in the mouth. Each sound is known as a phoneme and requires different muscles in the mouth, tongue, and lips to make the sound. The sound of "m," for example, requires the lips to be pressed together. Studying how people talk is critical to accurately modeling the character's mouth movements. Therefore, the rigger must find the places in the lips and face of the character where the mouth can be moved to make the sounds seem natural. Once the lips and face are rigged, the animator runs the character through all the sounds and stores the facial expressions in the computer's memory. Then, when the spoken dialogue is added, the animator can use the appropriate facial expression to match the phoneme uttered by the actor. Riggers will also look for other places in the face that may move to accompany a sound. They may rig an eyebrow to be raised when a character uses a curious tone, curl a lip if the dialogue requires the character to be sarcastic, or cause lines to appear in the character's forehead if he or she is upset.

Animators look to nature before they create animal images.

upright on its hind legs, it will be believable if it seems to have weight and presence in the scene."[10] What Weishar means is that rigging the character's movements is crucial in helping the audience focus on the film, rather than any inconsistencies in the animation techniques.

To do their jobs, riggers often find studying real-life examples to be helpful. The riggers who worked on the film *Ice Age* spent a lot of time at zoos, studying the motions of big cats so that they could properly plan the movements for Diego, the saber-toothed tiger. Weishar said, "When a tiger takes a simple step, a great deal more happens than just a leg moving forward. His tail may wag a bit, his pelvis will rotate, his back may curve, and various other parts of the body will shift to compensate for the redistribution of weight."[11] Being able to study movements of similar creatures in real life helps the riggers properly animate the movements on the computer.

ANIMATION

Once the characters have been properly modeled and rigged, it is time to make them move. This is the actual animation process. Generally, teams of animators are assigned to each scene. Their job is to bring life to the characters, manipulating their motions through each scene to tell the story that has been described in the script and storyboards.

In cel animation, the characters are given motion through a series of drawings, each slightly different than the last. When the cels are run through the camera at a high rate of speed, they fool the eye into believing that the character is alive on the screen. In computer animation, there is no need to provide thousands of images of the character in slightly different poses. Instead, the animator will select a few key poses and then direct the computer in providing the motions of the characters between those poses. To accomplish this task, the animator must tell the computer how much time needs to elapse from pose to pose and which joints in the temporary skeleton must be manipulated. The computer software will then move the splines or polygons according to this information.

There is no need to produce thousands of cel drawings, but animating through the computer is still an incredibly long and tedious process. At Pixar, for example, it has taken as long as five years to animate a single film, calling on the talents of hundreds of modelers, riggers, and animators, as well as software engineers and other technical staff members. Sometimes, as in the case of manipulating Sulley's 2.3 million hairs, the engineers had to design new software simply for that one task. Weishar said, "There are thousands of details involved in every shot. Whether it is a subtle movement of the eyes, or perhaps a shift in weight that gives the character more presence in a scene, an animator can tweak a single shot for weeks."[12] In animation, a scene cannot simply be re-shot if something looks off or unnatural, since the characters are just data and images stored in a computer. An animator must perfect each movement to create a seamless transition throughout each scene, which often means that a lot of trial and error occurs in the making of a character's movements and actions.

At this point, the characters may have been modeled, rigged, and animated, but the movie is far from finished. There are many other components that must be added before the film is ready for the theaters.

SETTING THE SCENE

In live-action filmmaking, the sets are generally illuminated by huge lights that shine on the actors. Properly lighting a film set is a craft practiced by skilled tradespeople who must know how to make actors look natural, how to avoid projecting unflattering light, and how to create the mood the director is seeking. Since computer animation requires artificial light created through the computer, an animator must spend a lot of time making it look natural.

There is a major difference in lighting a live-action film set and lighting a computer animation. To light a film set, the lamps are positioned off set and are shone onto the actors—the lamps themselves do not appear on film, only their light. On an animation screen, the animator cannot shine a computer-generated light onto the characters, because that light

Understanding light and shadow is as important to animators as it is to filmmakers.

source would show up on screen. Therefore, the animator must light each character and all other components of the scene by manipulating the color and intensity of each element in the scene. It must all be coordinated so that the lighting appears to be natural. Though lighting does not seem as important as the other aspects of the film, being able to tell the difference between day and night—or even sunny days and cloudy days—is a huge part in making a film look seamless and natural.

In addition to adjusting the lighting, backgrounds must be composed for all the scenes. In traditional cel animation, an artist would paint a static scene on which the cels are placed and photographed. In computer animation, the background scenes often feature three-dimensional aspects; likewise, the viewpoints shift as the characters move through them. Still, the first step in the process of designing backgrounds requires artists to paint two-dimensional images. These images will help the computer animators design backgrounds, sticking to the concepts for the scenes that have been worked out in advance.

The final step in the process is to convert the images stored on the computer onto film, which is the only way it can be shown in theaters. In cel animation, a movie camera is aimed at the cels, which are placed in front of the lens and are filmed one frame at a time. Converting computer-animated images to film is a much more intricate process, requiring special equipment that captures the computer's digital images onto 35mm film stock. However, animators do have a role in this process. As the images are recorded on film, the animators can watch the conversion on a monitor and adjust color, light, sharpness, and other features of the images as they are transferred.

CHAPTER FOUR

MOVIE MAGIC

The ultimate goal of animation is the goal of all movies: to tell a story through art. This idea is conceived in a variety of different ways. For example, in the movie *Inside Out*, the storyline follows a young girl and the feelings and thoughts that happen inside of her head, portrayed by little people that represent each emotion. The actual human characters—the girl and her family—are animated people that are meant to look, act, and move like animated people. The characters in the young girl's head, representing her emotions, are loosely based on the aspects of a person, but they have more exaggerated features and bodies composed of different colors and shapes. The features of each character are part of the story. For example, the characters are different colors, with each color corresponding to the idea of that emotion. Sadness, for instance, is blue, because people frequently refer to being sad as "feeling blue."

There is no question that the characters are animations; even the people who are meant to portray humans look like animations and not real-life people. This is the biggest distinction between animation and computer-generated imagery—CGI is meant to trick the audience into believing that what they are seeing onscreen—whether that is a person, a place, an animal, or something else—is real and not a 3D-animated form.

For years, animators and filmmakers have worked to find a process that makes animation look like real life. This process, which requires the talent of many artists and engineers, took a long time to develop. Today, we see films that feature humans and creatures that move as naturally as if they were real. This process allows live-action films to push the boundaries of reality and enhance their storylines.

LIFELIKE ANIMATION

Early cel animators attempted to create forms that looked and moved like real people. Since cel animation was essentially a large number of drawings screened together quickly, movements of characters could seem unnatural and jerky. In some cases this could work with the style of the movie; for example, Mickey Mouse's movements in *Steamboat Willie* are not typically criticized as not being "lifelike enough." However, when it came to movies with human characters, animators needed to find ways to lead each character throughout the scene more naturally.

This is a drawing showing a rotoscope patent design.

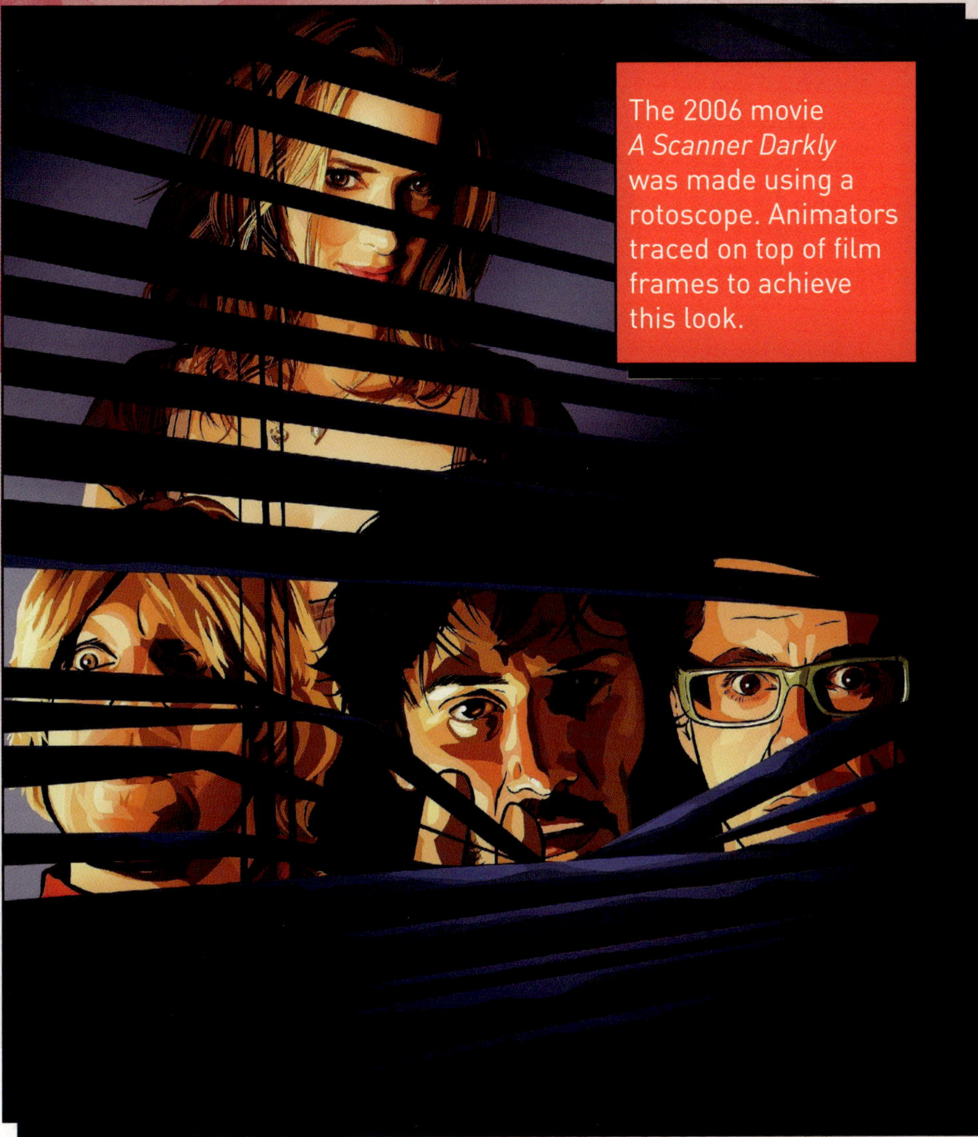

The 2006 movie *A Scanner Darkly* was made using a rotoscope. Animators traced on top of film frames to achieve this look.

The earliest attempts at this began with a process known as rotoscoping, which was a technique first used in 1914 by animator Max Fleischer. Fleischer built a projector, which he called a rotoscope, to display a series of filmed images on a screen composed of frosted white glass. Then he traced over the images, frame by frame, to create a cartoon.

In 1937, nearly a decade after animating the first adventures of Mickey Mouse, Disney produced the film *Snow White and the Seven Dwarfs*. The producers hoped to instill a sense of realism in the film by rotoscoping some of the characters. In Snow White's case, dancer Marge Champion served as the model for the princess. For some scenes, the animators studied her as she acted out the scenes and copied her movements into drawings. In other scenes, rotoscoping allowed them to project a film of Champion and directly trace over it so Snow White was holding the exact same poses. Cel animators continued trying different variations of these studies to help their characters look more lifelike.

Following the success of *Snow White and the Seven Dwarfs*, Disney released *Cinderella* in 1950, *Alice in Wonderland* in 1951, and *Sleeping Beauty* in 1959. In each movie, rotoscoping was used for some scenes, especially ones featuring dancing, which was difficult to animate well. Martin Goodman said, "Disney's films continued to feature human protagonists and typically did not falter in doing so. As realism and naturalism became desirable goals, the human figure was a proving ground for animators."[13]

CAPTURING MOVEMENT

Although rotoscoping was a groundbreaking technology and is still used in many cases today, it is time-consuming and tedious. Another common and effective way to achieve the look of a real person in animation is through a process called motion capture. To perform motion capture, an actor wears a suit containing hundreds of reflective sensors, which are mostly sewn into the joints but also appear elsewhere on the costume. As the actor moves, the camera reads the light reflected by the sensors, thus making a digital record of the actor's motions and turning them into a sort of skeleton. More broadly, this process is referred to as performance capture, since the person wearing the suit must act out each movement the animated character will need to make. This process also includes the capturing of facial expressions. After the actor performs each movement in a scene, the

Motion capture suits help animators produce realistic movements.

information is transferred to the computer, allowing the animator to paint over the skeleton with the art for the character.

The 2002 film *The Lord of the Rings: The Two Towers* made extensive use of motion capture to animate the character of Gollum, a corrupted hobbit who leads Frodo on his quest to destroy the powerful One Ring. Gollum was a CGI character, but he was animated through the use of motion capture. The filmmakers dressed actor Andy Serkis in a motion-capture suit and had him portray Gollum in all the scenes. Then, the filmmakers used motion capture to animate Gollum, matching his motions up perfectly to those made by Serkis. Finally, Gollum was digitally inserted into the movie's scenes accordingly.

Facial recognition software is used for motion capture as well. The movie *Avatar*, which broke the boundaries between live acting and animation, used facial expression motion capture to home in on the feelings of the animated characters. This film follows its main character, Jake, to another world where all of its inhabitants are blue, alien-like creatures. Live acting is used for the scenes where Jake is portrayed in the real world, and animation is used for the creatures on Pandora. For this animation to be achieved, 52 small green sensors were placed on the faces of the actors. Tiny cameras were held directly in front of their faces to capture each muscle movement. The actors then played out the scenes with each other. Since the sensors translated to the computer so quickly, the production team was able to film the characters around the virtual scene on their computer.

FULLY ANIMATED THROUGH MOTION CAPTURE

Although *The Lord of the Rings: The Two Towers* and the other films in the Lord of the Rings and the Hobbit series are full of CGI effects, the films are still essentially live-action movies. In 2004, Castle Rock Entertainment released *The Polar Express*, a computer-animated film made entirely through the motion-capture process. The film, based on a children's book written in 1985 by author and illustrator Chris Van Allsburg,

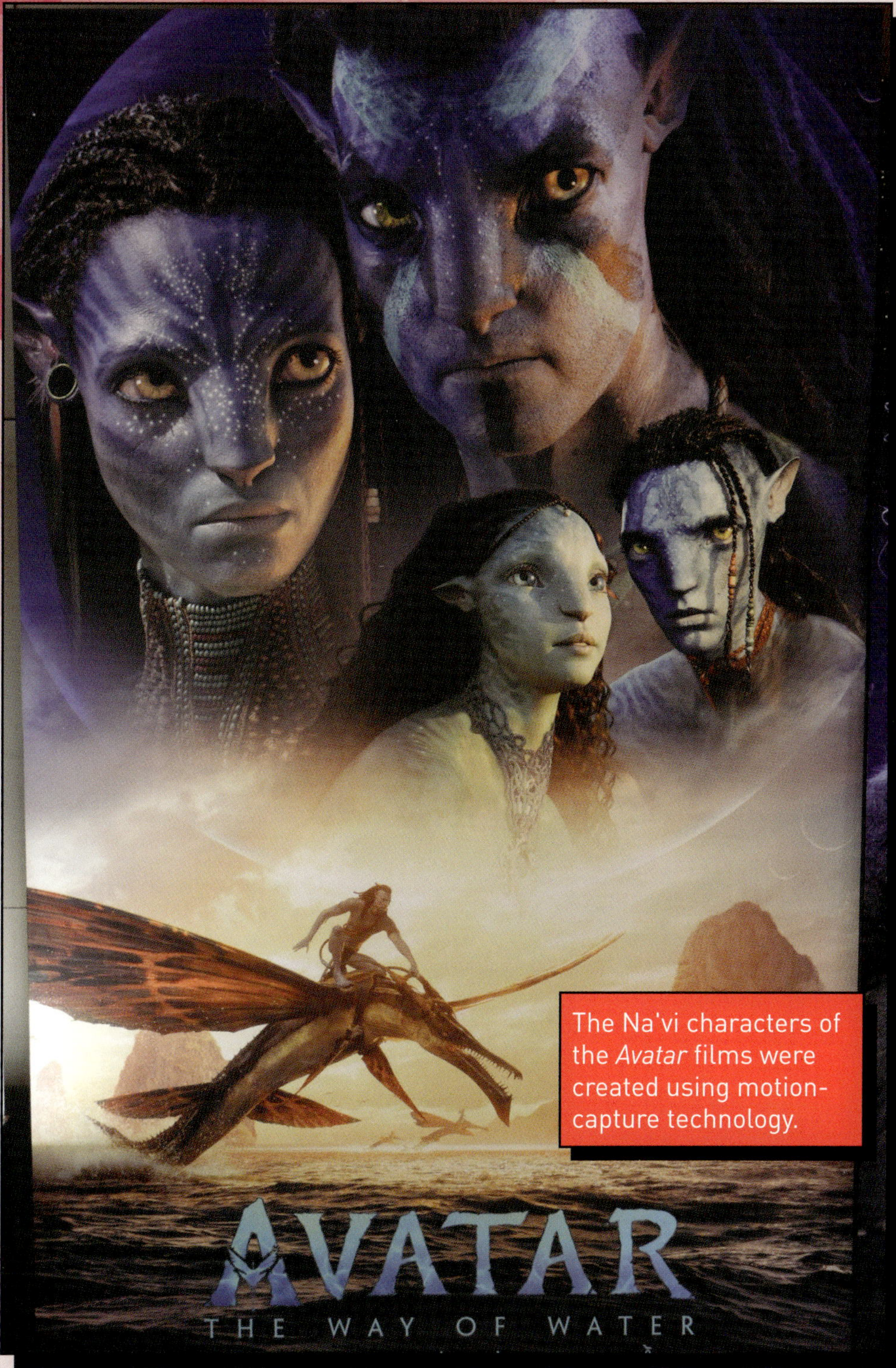

The Na'vi characters of the *Avatar* films were created using motion-capture technology.

MOCAP SUITS

Motion capture suits, or "mocap suits" as they are called by film industry professionals, have come a long way since the early 2000s. In the past, the suits were bulky and heavy because of all the large sensors, also called markers, on them. Today, there are two main kinds of suits available: marker-based and markerless. While the marker-based suits still have markers on them, they are lighter and more flexible than the ones that were first invented. Markerless suits, as the name suggests, do not have physical markers on them. This makes them easier to move in and faster to set up, but the result is less precise. An actor may use a marker-based suit for scenes that involve conversation or subtle movements and a markerless suit for action scenes.

Mocap suits have become standard in the video game industry. While not every game-maker uses them, especially independent game designers with lower budgets, they are frequently used by large studios. This is especially true of marker-based suits. Because of the physical sensors, the suits are more expensive and need to be set up by an expert who knows where to place the markers. Both types of suits also need the right software to go with them.

The markers, or sensors, on a mocap suit help the software pick up an actor's movements.

tells the story of a young boy who loses his faith in Santa Claus. On Christmas Eve, a magical train called the Polar Express appears at the boy's home and whisks him to the North Pole, where he meets Santa. At the North Pole, the boy finds a huge mechanized factory, rather than a quaint storybook workshop where elves make toys by hand. When the boy arrives, Santa selects him to receive the first gift of Christmas—a bright silver bell from Santa's sleigh. To make the film, director Robert Zemeckis elected to use the process of motion capture to animate all the characters.

Six of the characters, including the train's conductor and Santa Claus, were portrayed by Tom Hanks, who donned the motion-capture suit and performed all six roles in front of a blank screen. Zemeckis pointed out that acting a role in a motion capture suit can be far more difficult than playing a role on the stage in front of an audience. For example, when the part requires the actor to handle a prop, the actor has to go through the motions required in the script without the actual prop in his or her hands. "I believe the only thing Tom missed was having the physical trappings of a costume," Zemeckis said. "He had to remember that the conductor wore glasses when he was the conductor and he had to remember to touch the bill of his cap or adjust his collar, which he would have done more instinctively if he had been actually wearing that wardrobe."[14]

Of course, the animators had a lot more work to do than just create and animate characters based on the movements of Hanks and the other actors. They had to concoct a whole universe of landscapes, backgrounds, and other features for the film that had to appear as real as if they were filmed for a live-action production. Zemeckis also insisted that the look of the film be based on the illustrations Van Allsburg painted for the book. Thus, before the first drawings were made for the film, the production company's artists traveled to Van Allsburg's boyhood home in Grand Rapids, Michigan, where they made sketches of the home and neighborhood, which they intended to use for the backgrounds in the film.

Even the costumes worn by the animated characters received special attention by the filmmakers. Ordinarily, the animators may be left on their own to concoct the costumes for the animated characters, but in this case, the filmmakers called in a Hollywood costume designer, who designed the costumes and then had them sewn and fitted to the actors. Of course, the actors did not wear the costumes during the motion-capture sequences. Instead, the costumes were scanned and their images were downloaded into the computers. They were modeled and rigged and placed on the animated characters, allowing them to flow and move naturally, just as they would on a real person.

Production of *The Polar Express* turned out to be a complicated and expensive undertaking. It took 4 years and an investment of $170 million to bring the 100-minute movie to the screen. Most film critics applauded the quality of the computer animation, but they also suggested that the filmmakers fell short of producing convincing depictions of humans. Though they did not resemble real humans, film critic Roger Ebert still found the characters endearing. He said, "The characters in *The Polar Express* don't look real, but they don't look unreal, either; they have a simplified and underlined reality that makes them visually magnetic."[15]

ANIMATING DOBBY

Though the animation style of *The Polar Express* did not achieve the look of real humans, breakthroughs in film were beginning to do so both with and without modern motion-capture techniques. A character called Dobby, an enslaved house elf from the Harry Potter series, first appeared in the second installment of the series, *Harry Potter and the Chamber of Secrets*. Dobby appears in the film for the first time as he warns Harry Potter of the dangers of returning to Hogwarts School of Witchcraft and Wizardry. Dobby's character is a small creature that is both bold and nervous. Onscreen, Dobby looked almost real, with convincing movements and details such as wisps of hair and translucent ears.

George Lucas's animation firm, Industrial Light and Magic, created Dobby for the film. Unlike Gollum, Dobby was

The *Harry Potter* character Dobby was mostly created using CGI technology.

not created using motion capture but instead was rendered entirely on the computer. The actor playing Harry, Daniel Radcliffe, acted the scenes with the house elf using a ball on a stick for reference. Dave Adams, the animation director of the film, said in an interview for *Computer Graphics World*, "He's photoreal, he's acting alongside Daniel Radcliffe, who plays Harry, and he exhibits the subtlety of a real actor. He's the new bar at ILM [Industrial Light and Magic] against which future characteristics will be compared."[16] Several different aspects came together to create such a memorable character. Software programs were created to achieve his lifelike skin, as well as lighting techniques that helped the creature appear convincing in a real-world setting.

As with all technology, people are constantly working to improve and update motion capture hardware and software. Manufacturers are promoting even lighter, more flexible suits; integration with webcams and smartphones to make mocap available even to moviemakers with limited budgets; and artificial intelligence (AI) to improve the realism of motion capture movements as they are translated to the screen.

AI can help "fill in" movements missed by mocap suits.

CHAPTER FIVE

BEYOND ENTERTAINMENT

The field of computer animation is growing by leaps and bounds, with many job opportunities on offer. Due to technological advances, computer-animated films, games, and television shows have dominated the entertainment industry for many years and will continue to do so. Animation is now so realistic in some cases that it looks nearly real. For example, in the PlayStation game *Horizon: Zero Dawn*, the character of Aloy is so realistically animated that she has freckles, wrinkles, and peach fuzz visible on her face. The processes that allowed her to be so realistically portrayed continue to advance and shape the uses for and ideas behind computer animation. Animation, however entertaining, breaks the boundaries of just being functional for entertainment purposes, allowing computer animation techniques to be used in different aspects of everyday life. Now that people know how to manipulate something into a 3D form or sequence, other opportunities for this medium have been identified.

Computer-animated movies are among the most profitable films each year in the box office. The gaming industry continues to create thought-provoking games that provide hours of decision-making through scenarios with characters that appear nearly real. Furthering these advancements has taken significant amounts of time and creativity over the years. However, animation now also serves a purpose beyond entertainment. Medical professionals are now able to look at detailed 3D renderings of body parts to help further their learning on specific topics. Architects and designers now have the opportunity to flesh out a project through animation before beginning construction. Virtual reality (VR) headsets are available that allow a player's physical movements to alter a game or, in some instances, make them feel as if they are in actual, real-world places by providing a 360-degree viewpoint. Marketing techniques use animation to captivate consumers and to further explain the use and purpose of a product or service. Animation is part of many aspects of the world, and its applications continue to expand each day.

ADVERTISING AND ANIMATION

Marketing teams use animation in many aspects of product and service advertising. From television commercials to online marketing videos, animation is a key aspect in both gaining the attention of a consumer and accurately describing the product to them. Many brands have created a quirky spokesperson for their product. This spokesperson is featured in ads targeting a specific audience. A common animated character in commercial marketing techniques is the GEICO Gecko. Others include the M&M characters, the Pillsbury Doughboy, and Mr. Peanut.

Another example of successful marketing using animation comes from the world of technology. Apple is a very popular brand. Founded by Steve Wozniak and the late Steve Jobs, this tech company is one of the world's most recognizable brands. This is due in part to its successful marketing techniques, which sometimes include animated videos of each product. Apple products can also help people—even amateurs—create their own animations, and Apple does not miss the opportunity to advertise this capability. One 2024 ad called "Worlds Made on iPad" features three very different styles of animation done by three different artists with the same green screen footage of actress Sofia Wylie.

One Apple video advertising campaign, which features the company's new health application, has proved to be well-received among consumers. This set of simple, educational videos features a mix of real-world shots of ordinary items, such as

VR headsets offer users a 3D animation experience.

bikes and fruit, that seamlessly blend into animated segments of similar images.

The purpose of the video is to show the importance of monitoring health and the ways in which Apple's app can help consumers achieve their goals. It achieves this in a memorable way through the use of animation. Animation techniques such as this one play a crucial role in creating marketing material that is captivating enough to get people interested in a brand and its products.

ANIMATION IN OTHER PROFESSIONS

Architects and interior designers sometimes use computer animation to provide virtual tours for their clients, showing them how their new homes will look, inside and out, from various angles and points of view. In contrast to looking at a blueprint, these animations can essentially walk a person virtually through a new building or home, providing the option to choose between specific architectural choices and showing how the structure will come together as a whole. As new

Billboards can be animated to look like people or objects are emerging from the screen.

Architectural animation software can help architects create realistic 3D models of their designs.

Three-dimensional rendering can help homeowners design rooms in their homes.

construction is often expensive and time-consuming, being able to take a virtual walk-through of the building can help clients make changes early on. Modeling an animated home for a client is essentially no different than modeling a scene in a movie. When architects design a project for a client, they often do not have to start from scratch. They may have already stored images of walls, doors, windows, furniture, trees, and other features into their computers' memories. For example, instead of modeling a new door for every room in the house, they can simply drop the images into the animation wherever the plans call for a door, adjusting visual properties as needed.

Large architectural and design firms may employ their own animators. For small, simple projects, some architects and designers may be able to build the animation on their own using hardware and software specifically designed for modest animations. For something more complicated, many architectural and design firms are likely to retain the services of animation studios that specialize in providing architectural animations. "We've found that it takes a team of people to do what we're doing," said Joseph Bayer, president of an Ohio-based animation studio that specializes in architectural work. "We have someone who models, someone who does the actual texturing, lighting and animation paths, and someone else who does the video editing."[17] Being able to create an animation of a home or project before construction begins allows the architect to look through the structure to make adjustments and to fix any problems that may arise during construction. It also gives the people commissioning the building a chance to request changes or propose new ideas before the structure is even started. This saves time and money; for instance, it is expensive to knock down a wall after it is built, but it costs nothing to remove that wall from a virtual model.

In addition to architects and designers, other professionals who can make use of computer animation are doctors and medical students. Several animation studios now specialize in providing animated views of human anatomy, as well as animated run-throughs of surgical procedures. These 3D animations give students the opportunity to not only become familiar with each organ and body part inside and out, but also help them recognize the effects diseases have on organs such as the heart, lungs, and liver. Surgeons faced with difficult operations have made use of animated run-throughs, helping them decide which techniques to employ when they actually cut into their patients, as well as which problems might arise during the procedure. Pharmaceutical companies have commissioned animations to show how their drugs affect areas of the body.

Hybrid Medical Animation, a medical animation studio based out of Minneapolis, Minnesota, provides medical professionals with animations that give in-depth, and often interactive, 3D views of specific organs and bodily processes. In 2015, they created a 3D interactive animation of each part of the brain. The animation moves as the student or professional clicks around it, offering different options to further inspect the inside chambers of the brain. Since being able to sift through each part of the brain is something that is not readily available to students, being able to click through an animation that represents an exact replica is an incredible tool to help students and practicing professionals get a clear understanding of the

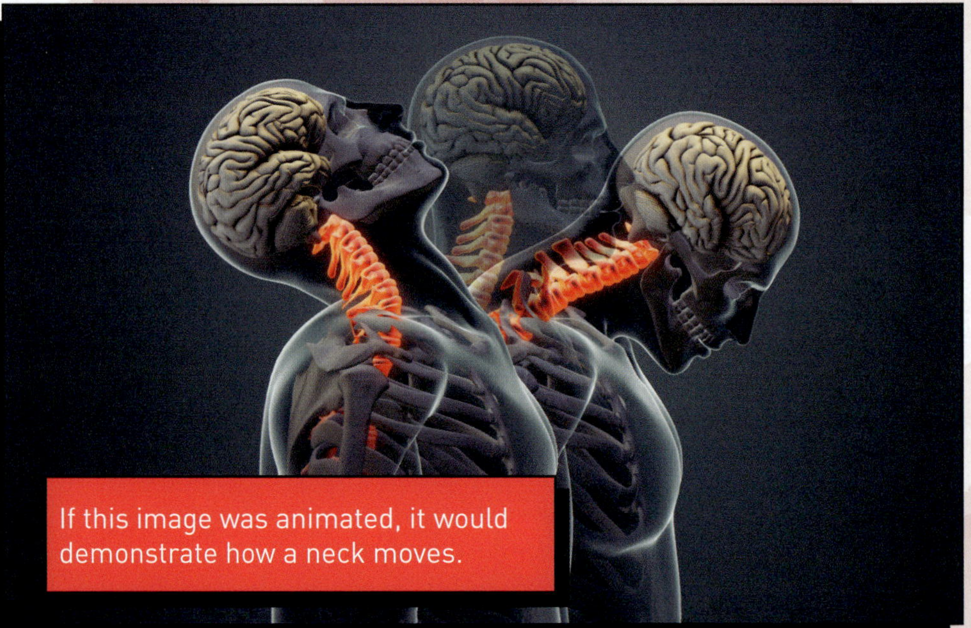

If this image was animated, it would demonstrate how a neck moves.

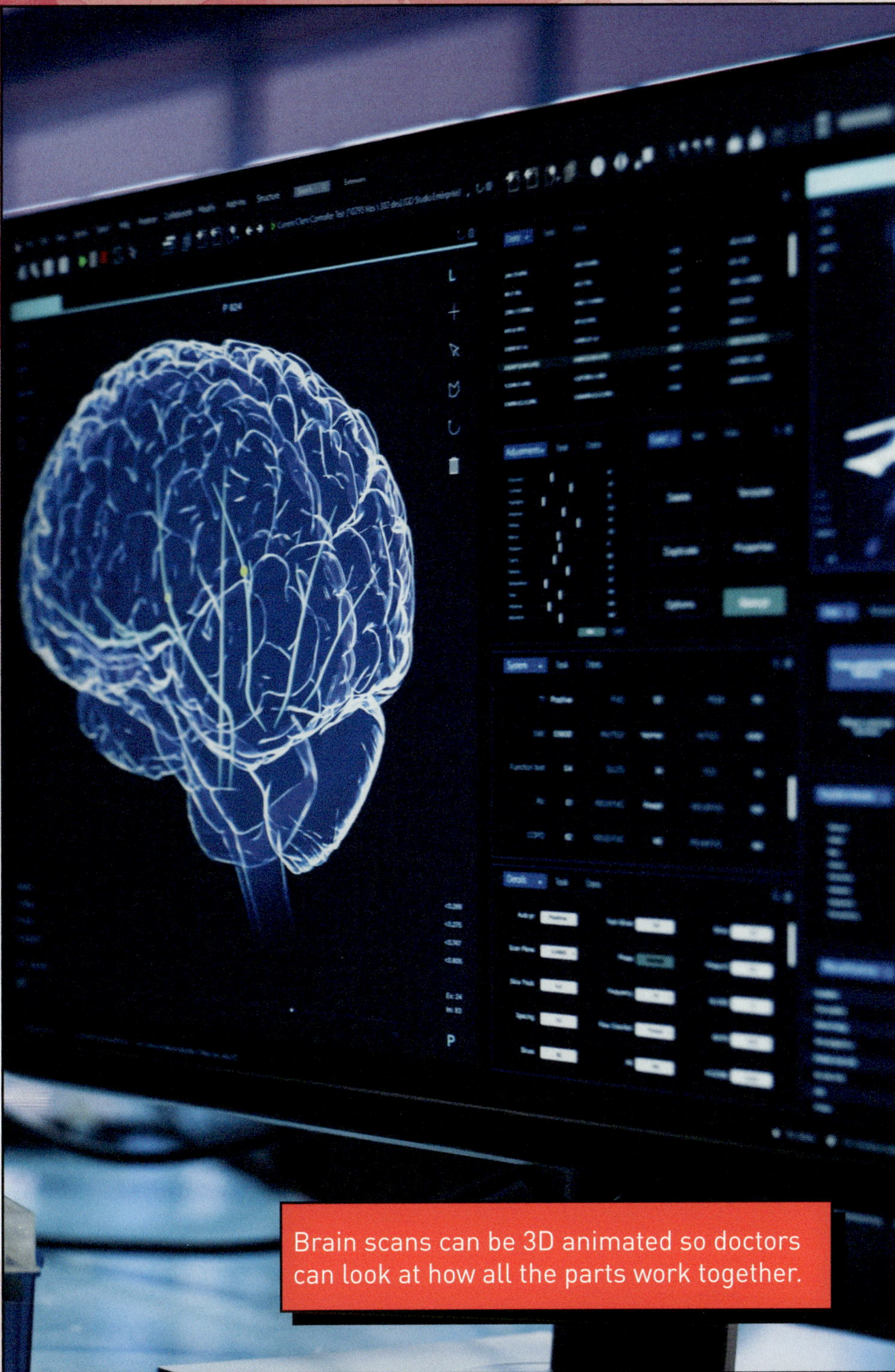

Brain scans can be 3D animated so doctors can look at how all the parts work together.

organ. This company has also ventured into using virtual reality as a tool to further their animations. Students are now able to see 360-degree views of internal organs and ways they are altered, giving them a front-row seat to each process as the animation progresses through the body.

Doctors, physical therapists, and sports trainers have made use of motion-capture technology to determine whether patients recovering from injuries were slowing their recoveries because of the way they walked, ran, or used their limbs. This tool is also used by athletes to determine how to adjust their skills to better achieve their goals or prevent injuries. One place where motion-capture technology has been used to study sports injuries is Boise State University, which has established a computer animation studio across the street from the school's football stadium.

Athletes who participate in the program wear motion-capture sensors on their bodies and are filmed running on a treadmill and performing other exercises by six cameras that record light reflected by the sensors. Animators then build models

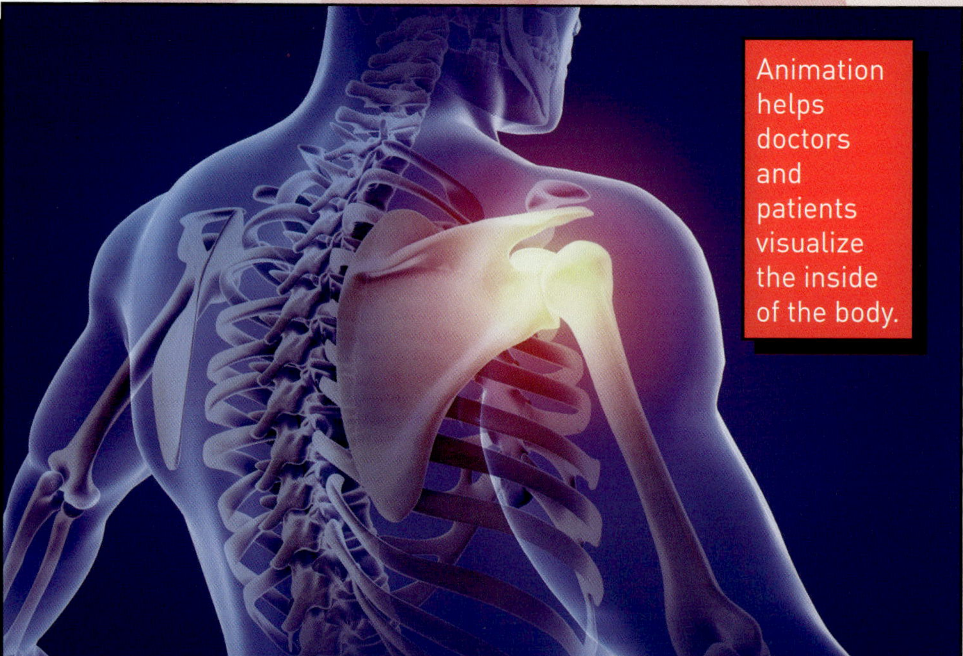

Animation helps doctors and patients visualize the inside of the body.

Animation software can help athletes see how their movements look so they can adjust where necessary.

Many golfers study their movements to improve. Animation of their swings can help.

of the athletes in their computers, using their body motions as guides—similar to how Tom Hanks was animated in *The Polar Express*.

By studying the animations, the Boise State researchers can tell whether a foot injury may be aggravated by the way an athlete lands on the balls of his or her feet or whether pitchers or quarterbacks may be aggravating their shoulder injuries by the way they throw. "There's still a lot we don't know about the factors that contribute to sports injuries," said Michelle Sabick, a biomedical researcher at Boise State. "It's a fascinating field of study."[18]

The Boise State researchers are also using motion-capture animation for more than just diagnosing sports injuries. Animation provides doctors and researchers a means of being able to home in on a specific action or skill and analyze ways that the player can improve upon it, such as a golf swing. Another service that Boise State offers is using animation

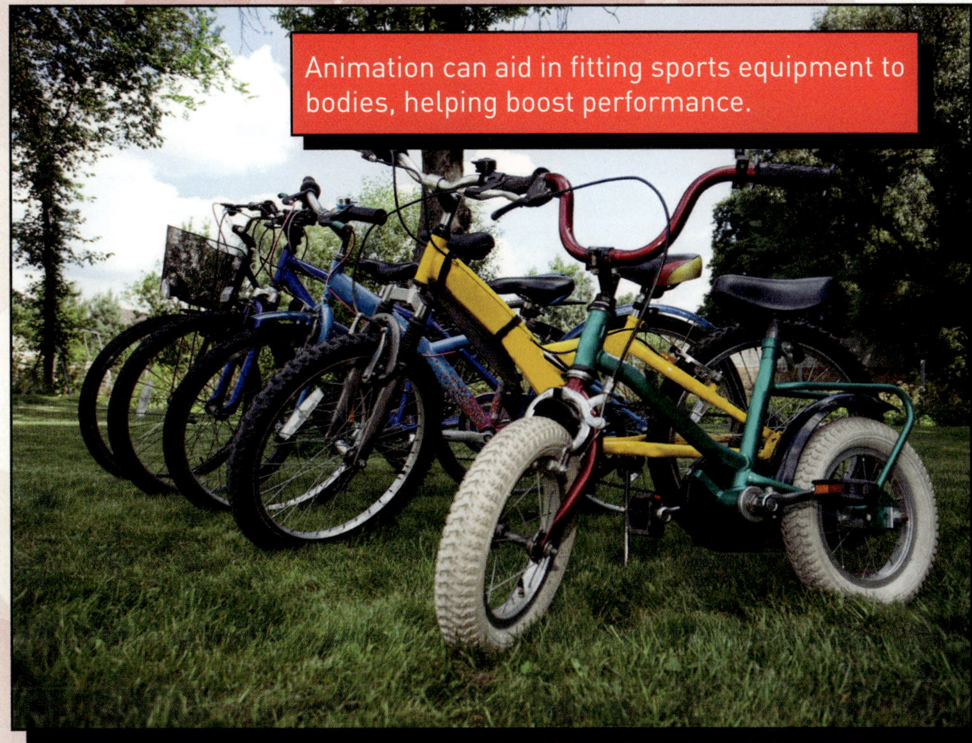

Animation can aid in fitting sports equipment to bodies, helping boost performance.

techniques to perfectly fit a bike to a person's body so that they can adjust each specific part to match their needs and riding techniques. As the technology behind animation expands, its applications in sports medicine and the way it can improve both an injury and a skill are expanding.

Using motion capture also allows doctors to analyze a patient after a major health problem, such as a stroke. By capturing a patient's movements and transferring them into animations on a computer for study, doctors are able to compare and contrast ways in which their mobility can be improved. Through studying the movements of a healthy, fully mobile person, doctors are able to track

Accident investigators use 3D animation to demonstrate how events may have happened.

This athlete uses motion-caption sensors to record her movements and, perhaps, to improve in her sport.

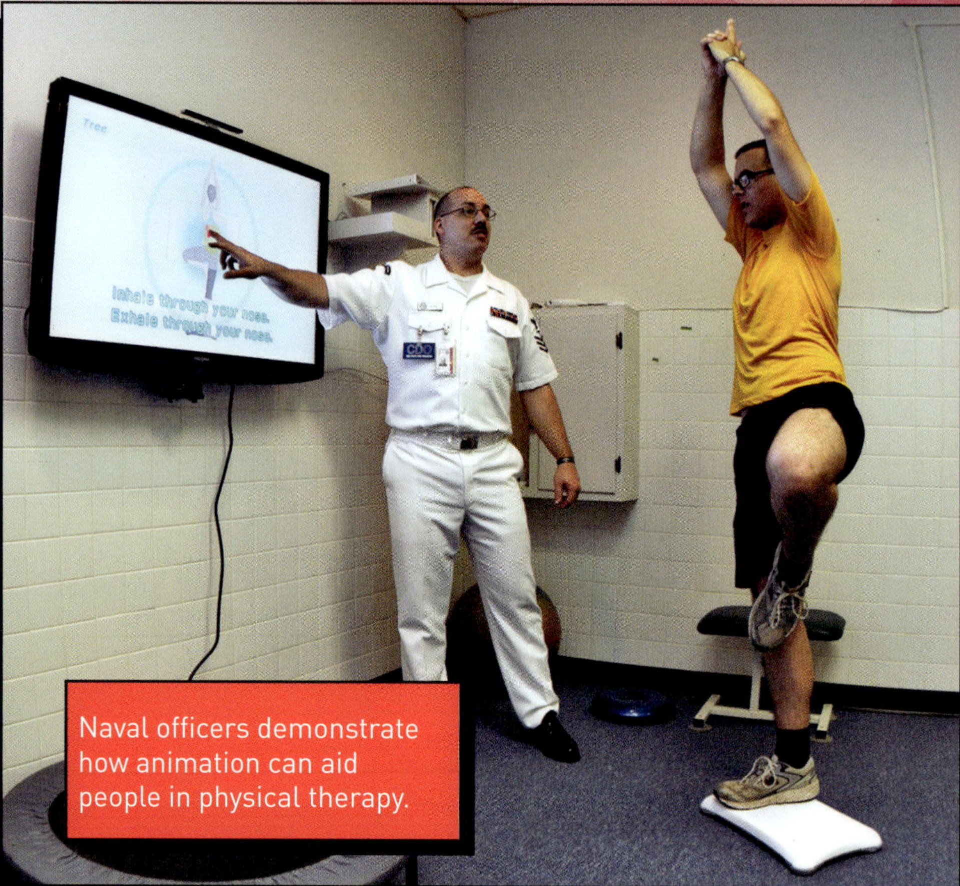

Naval officers demonstrate how animation can aid people in physical therapy.

specific joint movements and progress in the stroke patient, helping to find ways in which they can further extend their rehabilitation.

In sports medicine, animation is used as an investigative tool, allowing medical professionals to further research a topic or condition in order to find ways to better treat it. Attorneys have found that computer animation can be used as an investigative tool as well. They have employed it to simulate car collisions in cases where one or both parties involved are being sued. The animated simulations show all the important details of the accident, including a depiction of the scene, the weather conditions, the directions the cars were traveling, and other factors that may have caused the collision. Animators take the data provided to them by witnesses and court records and create a brief movie that juries can view to determine guilt and fix monetary damages. Several cases have been won due to a convincing animation that proves the other person guilty.

THE RISE OF VR

In addition to the progression of animation itself over the years, the vehicles through which animations are presented have changed as well. One huge breakthrough in animation is the use of virtual reality headsets. These headsets allow the user to control a game or setting using their own actions, while viewing the game or film through a headpiece that covers their face, allowing them to only see the screen in front of them. The idea behind virtual reality headsets is to seamlessly merge the experience with the technology, making the viewer feel like they are part of the animated world in front of them. As the player moves, their headset tracks those movements and moves the animation along with their motions. Since gaming and film are primarily focused on the scene in front of the player, allowing a full range of motion opens up a whole new realm of possibilities to animators. It also allows for more unique gameplay. For example, in a game called *Superhot*, time stops when the player stops moving their body.

Creating an experience wherein the viewer is able to view the entire conceived scene, not just the viewpoint in front of them, allows animators to create an entire animated world in 360-degree view. As the viewer turns, the scene turns, as if they were standing in the middle of it. Virtual reality films have become popular over the past few years. One film in particular, titled *Henry*, won an Emmy award in September of 2016. This animated tale featuring a hedgehog that throws itself a birthday party was created by one of the top virtual reality companies, Oculus. The company employed a separate division, Story Studio, which is devoted to creating virtual reality films. Several well-known animators, many who have contributed to the production of the top animated movies, created *Henry*. The first scene of the film shows Henry's home. Viewers standing with the virtual headset on are able to physically walk around, exploring each detail of the tiny hedgehog's home, including being able to lean in and get a closer look at things. Ramiro Lopez Dau, the director of *Henry* and an animator on the movie *Monsters University*, said in an interview with the *Los Angeles Times*, "What feels normal in traditional film feels fast here, and what feels boring in traditional film feels good here … In VR, we're learning that you don't need a character to do as much to be interesting."[19] Being able to physically move through an animated space allows the viewer to focus more on the details of the setting and characters, homing in on small details of the film that would be otherwise impossible to see in normal films.

A REANIMATED BODY

One of the most interesting and controversial breakthroughs in animation occurred in the Star Wars film *Rogue One: A Star Wars Story*. The film touched upon scenes and characters from the first Star Wars film, released in 1977, because it took place right before the events of that first film. The directors decided that some scenes required the use of previous characters from past films to further connect the storylines. One character in particular is Grand Moff Tarkin, known as the commander of the Death Star. The actor who played him, Peter Cushing, passed away in 1994. The filmmakers were faced with a decision: explain why the commander of the Death Star was not part of a scene that specifically involves him, cast a different actor, or create a CGI version of Cushing. They chose the last option.

Industrial Light and Magic hired an actor and had him act out each necessary scene in a motion capture outfit. From there, they uploaded everything onto a computer and began the process of what creative officer John Knoll referred to as "a super high-tech and labor-intensive version of doing make-up."[20] Using scenes that Cushing had acted out in previous films, the creators were essentially able to digitally paint his

Pokémon Go combines animation and the real world, making it look like a Pokémon is in front of the user.

face onto the actor's body for each scene. Several aspects of this process proved difficult; factors such as lighting and the stand-in actor's mouth movements differed from the original footage.

Another problem the team encountered was what has been dubbed "the slipper problem." When he was filming his scenes in the original movies, Cushing reportedly wore slippers on the set because the boots he was provided with fit poorly and hurt his feet. For this reason, there were no shots of his feet and very few of his legs. Animators needed these to make the CGI Cushing walk convincingly. Some of those shots were ultimately taken from other movies Cushing had been in.

Despite these problems, the team succeeded in creating believable scenes with the commander of the Death Star, seemingly placing an actor who had long since passed into new footage. While it was widely acknowledged that the feat was impressive, some people felt that this move was disrespectful to the actor's memory and that dead people should not be used this way. Others pointed out that although the CGI Cushing looked real in photos, it was a little disorienting to watch it try to interact with other actors in the movie.

The studio ran into a more serious problem than negative public opinion: It was sued by one of Cushing's friends, who stated that Lucasfilm, now owned by Disney, did not have the legal right to recreate Cushing. Lucasfilm also did not pay Cushing's estate any money for the use of his image until the studio was contacted with a request for payment. Lucasfilm tried twice, unsuccessfully, to have the lawsuit dismissed. As of 2024, the case was still ongoing, with no new updates in 2025.

THE NEXT GENERATION OF ANIMATORS

Becoming skilled in computer animation takes many years of perfecting multiple skills. Though there are many different types of animators, each one shares the same fundamental skills. One of the most important skills needed to become a good animator is drawing. It is important to understand how people, animals, and objects are constructed to be able to make them move on a computer. Understanding how to translate those movements into 2D and 3D drawings is a crucial first

Peter Cushing's likeness was used in a *Star Wars* movie after he died, leading to controversy and fundamental questions about image ownership.

step in animation. Another important skill is understanding the computer programs used to create an animation. Many different software programs are required to successfully execute an animation, and understanding how to efficiently and accurately navigate through them is an important skill.

Ringling College of Art and Design in Florida is ranked third best in the United States for its animation program. Savannah College of Art and Design is ranked second, and California Institute of the Arts is ranked first. Aside from several animation-based classes, the curriculum for Ringling's four-year program includes drawing and figure drawing classes, as well as classes in 2D and 3D design. Many other colleges and universities around the country offer excellent programs in computer animation as well. Some are more specifically geared toward a particular skill, such as medical and forensic animation. If someone decides to pursue a career in computer animation, finding a good program to help them perfect their knowledge and skills can be very helpful.

The history of animation has progressed such a great deal that there is no telling where it will lead in the future. The industry has come a long way since the beginnings of cel animation in filmmaking. Today's animations are sometimes nearly indistinguishable from real people at first glance, while remakes of old cel animation films using computer animation can offer audiences a different perspective on a familiar story from a technologically new standpoint. Animation is everywhere, providing entertainment and selling new products. Its evolution has advanced rapidly, and new techniques are being developed continually.

NOTES

INTRODUCTION: ANIMATION ADVANCEMENTS

1. Brent Schlender, "Interview with Steve Jobs," *Fortune*, September 18, 1995. archive.fortune.com/magazines/fortune/fortune_archive/1995/09/18/206099/index.htm.

CHAPTER ONE: ANIMATION OVER TIME

2. Charles Solomon, *Enchanted Drawings: The History of Animation*. New York, NY: Wings, 1994, p. 40.
3. Quoted in Paul Trachtman, "Charles Csuri Is an 'Old Master' in a NewMedium," *Smithsonian Magazine*, February 1995, p. 56
4. Quoted in Joe Tracy, "An Inside Look at the Original Beauty and the Beast," *Digital Media FX Magazine*. www.digitalmediafx.com/Beauty/Features/originalbeauty.html.

CHAPTER TWO: A SHORT HISTORY OF GAMES

5. Keith Ferrell, "Quiet on the Set: Interaction!," *Omni*, November 1991, p. 93.
6. Quoted in B.I. Koerner, "How Pong Invented Geekdom," *U.S. News & World Report*, December 27, 1999, p. 67.
7. Quoted in David Sheff, *Game Over: How Nintendo Zapped an American Industry, Captured Your Dollars, and Enslaved Your Children*. New York, NY: Random House, 1993, p. 136.

CHAPTER THREE: A WORK IN PROGRESS

8. Quoted in John Horn, "Enough Pixels, Time for Comedy Class," *Newsweek*, April 29, 2002, p. 46.
9. Patrick Kriwanek, "Storytelling Through Cuts," *Animation Mentor Report*, October 2005. www.animationmentor.com/newsletter.1005/feature_storytelling.html.
10. Peter Weishar, *Blue Sky: The Art of Computer Animation*. New York, NY: Harry N. Abrams, 2002, p. 28.
11. Weishar, *Blue Sky*, p. 29.
12. Weishar, *Blue Sky*, p. 67.

CHAPTER FOUR: MOVIE MAGIC

13. Martin Goodman, "Dr. Toon: Running with the Pack," *AnimationWorld*, November 15, 2006. mag.awn.com/?article_no=3081.
14. Quoted in Julian Phillips, "Performance Capture CGI Techniques Makes 'The Polar Express' an Advance for Animation," *Skwigly Animation Magazine*, October 27, 2004. www.skwigly.co.uk/magazine/news/article.asp?articleid=346&zoneid=3.
15. Roger Ebert, "The Polar Express," *Chicago Sun-Times*, November 10, 2004. www.rogerebert.suntimes.com/apps/pbcs.dll/article?AID=/20041109/REVIEWS/41006005.
16. Audrey Doyle, "Pivotal Role," *Computer Graphics World*. Volume: 26 Issue: 2, February 2003. www.cgw.com/Publications/CGW/2003/Volume-26-Issue-2-Feb-2003-/Pivotal-Role.aspx.

CHAPTER FIVE: BEYOND ENTERTAINMENT

17. Diana Phillips Mahoney, "Moving Beyond CAD," *Computer Graphics World*, June 1997, p. 20.

18. Quoted in *Idaho Statesman*, "BSU Professor Studies Sports Injuries," December 17, 2006.
19. Steven Zeitchik, "With 'Henry,' a Cinematic Leap into World of Virtual Reality," *Los Angeles Times*, July 28, 2015. www.latimes.com/entertainment/movies/la-et-mn-oculus-vr-henry-20150728-story.html.
20. David Itzkoff, "How 'Rogue One' Brought Back Familiar Faces," *New York Times*, December 27, 2016. www.nytimes.com/2016/12/27/movies/how-rogue-one-brought-back-grand-moff-tarkin.html?_r=1.

FOR MORE INFORMATION

BOOKS

Ford, Jeanne Marie. *Movie Technology*. Parker, CO: The Child's World, 2024.

Readers discover more about the tech behind their favorite movies in this book.

Furgang, Adam. *Coding Activities for Making Animation and Art in Scratch*. New York, NY: Rosen Publishing, 2022.

This book allows readers to explore coding projects related to the world of animation.

Kallen, Stuart A. *Exploring Animation*. San Diego, CA: ReferencePoint Press, 2025.

Readers can learn more about all kinds of animation in this book.

Owen, Ruth, and John Willis. *CGI Artists*. New York, NY: AV2, 2021.

This book explores what a career as a CGI artist is like.

WEBSITES

Coder Kids: Animation Basics for Kids
www.coderkids.com/blog/animation-basics-for-kids

Although a computer is necessary to create computer animation, this website explains the basics with a flipbook tutorial.

Kiddle: Computer Animation Facts for Kids
kids.kiddle.co/Computer_animation

Learn more interesting facts about how computer animation works.

Monster Mash
monstermash.zone/#

This website lets visitors create a short animation of their own drawings.

Pixar
pixar.com

Learn more about upcoming Pixar films as well as some of the technology the company uses to create them.

YouTube: "Zoetropes Create 3D Illusions Using Light"
www.youtube.com/watch?v=40__creuq7c

This video shows how a device called a zoetrope creates an animation effect using light, motion, and 3D sculptures. The artist featured in this video uses animation software to map out the zoetrope's movements.

INDEX

I

J

K

L

M

PICTURE CREDITS

Cover Gorodenkoff/Shutterstock.com; Cover, p. 1 robuart/Shutterstock.com; Cover, pp. 1-104 MOMO STOCK/Shutterstock.com; Cover, pp. 4, 6, 11, 31, 45, 59, 71, 93, 96, 98, 103, 104 ReVelStockArt/Shutterstock.com; p. 5 Hamara/Shutterstock.com; p. 7 RBM Vintage Images/Alamy.com; p. 9 cfg1978/Shutterstock.com; p. 10 https://commons.wikimedia.org/wiki/File:Joseph_Bau_House_Museum_04.jpg; p. 12 Dontree_M/Shutterstock.com; p. 15 Shazwany/Shutterstock.com; p. 16 catwalker/Shutterstock.com; p. 23 Photo 12/Alamy.com; p. 24 Scorpioda/Shutterstock.com; p. 26 Sarunyu L/Shutterstock.com; p. 27 Christian Bertrand/Shutterstock.com; p. 28 Usa-Pyon/Shutterstock.com; p. 30 tetesong/Shutterstock.com; p.33 https://commons.wikimedia.org/wiki/File:Spaceware!.jpg; p. 35 Tinxi/Shutterstock.com; p. 39 Logan Bush/Shutterstock.com; p. 40 fvgromanelli/Shutterstock.com; p. 42 MardeFondos/Shutterstock.com; p. 43 Miguel Lagoa/Shutterstock.com; p. 44 Miguel Lagoa/Shutterstock.com; p. 46 Cinematic/Alamy.com; p. 48 Mila Basenko/Shutterstock.com; p. 50 lmwrites/Shutterstock.com; p. 53 Frame Stock Footage/Shutterstock.com; p. 54 Mary Angela Heys/Shutterstock.com; p. 57 Pavel L Photo and Video/Shutterstock.com; p. 60 https://commons.wikimedia.org/wiki/File:US_patent_1242674_figure_3.png; p. 61 Maximum Film/Alamy.com; pp. 63, 66, 79 Gorodenkoff/Shutterstock.com; p. 65 Sarunyu L/Shutterstock.com; p. 69 Anton_Ivanov/Shutterstock.com; p. 70 Supamotionstock.com/Shutterstock.com; p. 73 Media_Photos/Shutterstock.com; p. 74 yllyso/Shutterstock.com; p. 75 DC Studio/Shutterstock.com; p. 76 MariaO97/Shutterstock.com; p. 78 JitendraJadhav/Shutterstock.com; p. 80 Cinefootage Visuals/Shutterstock.com; p. 81 Storyet/Shutterstock.com; p. 82 Photoongraphy/Shutterstock.com; p. 83 Ground Picture/Shutterstock.com; p. 84 Rahmat Syam/Shutterstock.com; p. 85 Jacob Lund/Shutterstock.com; p. 86 https://commons.wikimedia.org/wiki/File:US_Navy_090702-N-1783P-003_Hospital_Corpsman_1st_Class_Guy_Duke,_left,_and_Electronics_Technician_3rd_Class_Joshua_Benedict_demonstrate_how_the_Physical_therapy_Department_at_Naval_Health_Clinic,_Charleston_use_the_Wii_Fit%27s_yoga.jpg; p. 89 enchanted_fairy/Shutterstock.com; p. 91 catwalker/Shutterstock.com.

ABOUT THE AUTHOR

JUDY THORPE graduated from Fredonia College, where she received her Bachelor of Arts degree in both English and graphic design. She currently resides in Buffalo, New York, where she is both a writer and a designer.

Relámpagos
y nieve
por Sebastián Olaso
ilustraciones de Anita Morra

La familia
pingüino
por Luis Reyes
ilustraciones de Paul Meisel

Nuestro extraño planeta

por Sebastián Olaso
ilustraciones de Victoria Assanelli

Si te resulta extraño pensar en cosas como la gravedad, este artículo te brindará excelente información. Prueba de levantar un objeto. ¿Te parece pesado? Algunos objetos pesan menos que otros. Eso tiene que ver con la gravedad.

Sostén una piedra. Cierra la mano y extiende el brazo. Evita lastimarte. Ahora, abre los extremos de tus dedos para soltar la piedra y mira cómo cae. ¡Excelente, así se explica la gravedad!

Las extraordinarias fuerzas de la Tierra atraen los objetos hacia abajo. Si pruebas hacia los costados, no tendrás éxito. Una puerta no se cierra sola. La gravedad existe cuando se trata de levantar o de dejar caer, pero no de empujar y jalar.

Prueba con el próximo experimento:

Haz un avioncito de papel. Verás que vuela un poco y luego cae lentamente. Tarda algunos segundos en llegar abajo. Tarda más que la piedra porque es menos pesado. Pero eso no evita que cumpla exactamente con la ley de la gravedad.

Todas las cosas, sin excepción, son atraídas por las fuerzas que hay en el centro de la Tierra. Examinar la gravedad nos abre una puerta hacia el conocimiento de los extraños fenómenos que vemos todos los días. ¡Qué bueno, ya somos unos expertos!

En el cielo

por Leslie A. Rotsky

En una noche clara puedes desconectarte de la actividad y mirar el cielo. Fija tu rostro directamente hacia las estrellas. Entre la sombra y el silencio puedes expresar esto: “Enviaré un mensaje en cuanto vea que pasa una estrella fugaz, y mi sueño se cumplirá”.

NASA/ESA

¿Por qué las estrellas brillan en el cielo?

Las estrellas brillan porque están hechas de gases extremadamente calientes, que explotan y sus destellos y su sombra se extienden como producto de esas explosiones. Es correcto decir que brillan durante las veinticuatro horas del día, pero solo podemos observarlas durante la noche.

Stocktrek Images/Getty Images

¿Tienen las estrellas el mismo tamaño?

Las estrellas tienen diferentes tamaños. En efecto, algunas son más grandes que el Sol. ¡Y el Sol es muy, pero que muy grande! La distancia hace que lo veamos mucho más pequeño de lo que es.

¿Cuál es la estrella más cercana a la Tierra?

La estrella más cercana es el Sol. Lo vemos de manera clara y perfecta durante las horas del día. Sin la acción del Sol, nuestro planeta sería muy frío.

Roger Radtke

¿Qué imágenes forman las estrellas?

Con unas pocas estrellas y una imaginación activa podemos crear figuras con las estrellas. Podemos pasar horas mirando y creando imágenes, como un animal, una construcción o un rostro.

Una buena idea es tomar unos prismáticos en las horas de mayor silencio y pasar un rato imaginando figuras que parezcan extraídas de un sueño. Luego, podemos redactar un informe o un poema de pocas líneas para expresar lo que sentimos.

¿Cómo podemos espiar las estrellas?

Un telescopio como este es excelente para espiar la acción de las estrellas. Es muy divertido mirarlas y descubrir cómo se comportan. Y siempre recuerda que puedes expresar esto: "Enviaré un mensaje en cuanto vea que pasa una estrella fugaz, y mi sueño se cumplirá".

Steve Cole/Photodisc/Getty Images

Escoge tres deseos

por Sergio Foscale
ilustraciones de Valeria Cervantes

El gigante Javier tenía un jardín con muchas flores que debía proteger. Él no tenía empleados y hacía todo el trabajo.

—Gracias al modo de cuidarlas, se mantendrán frescas durante mucho tiempo —decía Javier.

“Un buen viaje es lo que desea un hombre como yo. Pero los viajes toman mucho tiempo”, pensaba Javier. Cruzó la calle que atraviesa el sector de los geranios y le preguntó a su amigo, el gigante Julián, si podía cuidar su jardín.

—Sí —dijo Julián—. Tus jazmines se mantendrán frescos bajo mi vigilancia.

Javier se alejó y en un carruaje atravesó anchos campos donde trabajaban muchos empleados.

Julián, su hijo y su señora eran personas que estaban dispuestas a ayudar.

Un día, la mujer encontró una vasija. Estaba sumergida en una zanja ancha.

La mujer quiso enjuagarla. Tomó jabón y la lavó. De pronto, salió un genio.

—Escoge tres deseos. Estoy aquí para hacer realidad lo que desea la gente buena —dijo de un modo muy amable.

Los ojos de la mujer se abrieron con sorpresa. Como era gentil y generosa, la buena señora pidió:

—Que la gente sea feliz. Que estemos todos juntos. Y... ¡que el viaje de Javier sea genial!

Relámpagos y nieve

por Sebastián Olaso
ilustraciones de Anita Morra

Las nubes ocupan un lugar en el cielo gris. El calor de la tarde se apaga. Se anuncia un posible aguacero con gruesas gotas. Gabriela y Guillermo juegan en la galería. Papá recién acabó de preparar un guiso especial para la cena.

Mientras engullen el guiso, ven por la ventana que un círculo oscuro rodea la luna. No se pueden ver las estrellas.

—¿Habrá nieve? —pregunta Gustavo.

—Es posible. Luego contaremos lo que es una alerta meteorológica —dice papá.

Ya acabó la cena. Mamá toma un libro que parece especial. A los niños les gusta una imagen gigante del desierto. Mamá dice que los meteorólogos investigan sobre el clima. Gabriela y Guillermo saben que en el desierto hace mucho calor.

Siempre con el libro como guía, mamá y papá explican que hoy seguramente no se verán estrellas en el cielo. Está demasiado oscuro y caen relámpagos. Ya comenzó a nevar. El viento azota la zona y agita el agua del lago.

Sin embargo, mamá y papá dicen que no deben temer ni a los relámpagos, ni al agua ni a la nieve. En este hogar están seguros. También están seguros la gata y los gatitos.

La familia pingüino

por Luis Reyes

ilustraciones de Paul Meisel

La Antártida tiene temperaturas bajo cero. El hielo es blanco como el papel. Cada día, los pingüinos Lila y Koda deben pasar una dura prueba de supervivencia. No tienen labios ni manos. Quieren pintar el paisaje con sus plumas brillantes.

Un día apareció una cigüeña cerca de ellos. Se inclinó hacia adelante para saludar. La cigüeña tampoco tiene manos ni labios. Tiene un pico fuerte y largo. Su presencia era un buen agüero. Y la halagüeña predicción no se hizo esperar.

La cigüeña les dejó un huevo. Había que darle calor y protección. Con muy buenos sentimientos, Lila lo cuidaba del agüita, del frío y de la nieve. Era como tener el huevo bajo un paragüitas. Era la imagen bella para pintar en un papel.

El gran día llegó. De pronto, el cascarón se rompió como un papel y apareció un pingüinito. Caminaba balanceándose hacia adelante. Su padre tenía buenos sentimientos. Le colocó un pescadito rico en la lengüita.

Lo llamaron Kokó. Con el tiempo, llegó la hora de nadar de un lado a otro.

—¡Haz la prueba, Kokó! —dijo su madre—. ¡No te asustes o avergüences! Los pingüinos nadan desde la antigüedad.

¡Y Kokó nadó muy feliz!

Unidad 3: Vivir y aprender

Semana 1: Nuestro extraño planeta *página 1*

para leer con *¡Imanes en acción!* **NÚMERO DE PALABRAS: 203**

PALABRAS CON X, LA X COMO J

exactamente, examinar, excelente, excepción, existe, éxito, expertos, extraño, extraordinarias, próximo

PALABRAS DE USO FRECUENTE

abajo, cae, cierra, cosas, eso, evita, levantar, menos, pesado, puerta

Semana 2: En el cielo *página 7*

para leer con *Viaje estelar* **NÚMERO DE PALABRAS: 307**

PALABRAS CON CC, X

acción, construcción, excelente, explosiones, explotan, expresar, expresar, extienden, extraídas, extremadamente

PALABRAS DE USO FRECUENTE

clara (adj.), enviaré, horas, mensaje, pasa, pocas, rostro, silencio, sombra, sueño

Semana 3: Escoge tres deseos *página 15*

para leer con *Iluminando vidas* **NÚMERO DE PALABRAS: 198**

PALABRAS CON GE, GI, J

bajo, enjuagarla, generosa, genio, gigante, hijo, jardín, ojos, proteger, viaje

PALABRAS DE USO FRECUENTE

ancho, atraviesa, calle, desea, empleados, mantendrán, modos (sus.), personas, señora, toman

Semana 4: Relámpagos y nieve

página 21

para leer con *¡Tornado!*

NÚMERO DE PALABRAS: 195

PALABRAS CON GA, GO, GU, GUE, GUI

agua, apaga, embargo, engullen, gatitos, guía, guiso, lago, pregunta (v.), seguros

PALABRAS DE USO FRECUENTE

acabó, calor, cielo, desierto (sus.), especial, estrellas, nieve, oscuro, posible, rodea

Semana 5: La familia pingüino *página 27*

para leer con *¡Ellos tienen ritmo!* **NÚMERO DE PALABRAS: 199**

PALABRAS CON DIÉRESIS GÜE, GÜI

agüero, agüita, antigüedad, avergüences, cigüeña, halagüeña, lengüita, paragüitas, pingüinito, pingüinos

PALABRAS DE USO FRECUENTE

adelante, bajo, labios, lado, manos, o (conj), papel, pintar, prueba, sentimientos

PALABRAS DE USO FRECUENTE APRENDIDAS HASTA LA FECHA

Grado K

al
con
dice
dónde
el
ella
en
es
está
este (adj)
familia
grande
gusta
hace
hago
hay
juego (v.)
la
más
mira
muy
nuevo
para
pequeño
pero
por
puedo
qué
quién
sin
soy
también
tengo
tiene
un
vamos
veo
voy
y
yo

Grado I

abrir
aceptar
actividad
agua
ahí
aire
algunos
allá
ambos
amigo
años
aprender
aquí
aspecto
atrás
aunque
ayuda
baja
bien
blanco
bueno
camino
campo
cantar
carácter
casa
casi
cerca
ciudad
clase
color
comer
como
completo
correr
crear
cualquier
cuando
cuanto
cuatro
cuerpo
cumplir
decidieron
dentro
después
diez
diferente
difícil
doctor
dos
durante
edad
embargo
empezar
encima
encontrar
entonces
entre
escribe
escuchar
escuela
esfuerzo
estoy
estudio (sust.)
existen
explicar
flores
frente
grupo
gusto
hablar
habrá
hacia
hoy
iguales
importante
juguemos
juntos
larga
lector
libertad
libro
llamar
lograr
luego
luz
madre
maestro
manera
mañana
mejor
mientras
mover
muchos
muestro
nada
nadie
niño
nombre
nuestro
obra
obtener
ocho
ofrece
otro
padre
palabra
pan
parque
piensa
podrás
porque
pregunta
presentar
primero
principal
principio
problema
pronto
propio
proponer
próximo
pueblo
puede
pues
que (cj.)
quien
quiere
quiero
quizá
reunir
río
saltar
saluda
seguir
siempre
siglo
sobre
sube
suelo
tampoco
tan
tiempo
tierra
todavía
todo
trabajo
trae
través
tres
varios
vez
vieja
vivir
voz
ya

Grado 2

abajo
acabó
adelante
ahora
alegría,
algo
algún
alto
aman
ancho
andará
animales
apenas
artista
atención
atraviesa
azul
bajo
bella
busca
cabeza
cae
calle
calor
canto (sus.)
cargan
carrera
cielo
cierra
clara (adj.)
coloca
comienzan
construyen
cosas
demasiado
desea
desierto (sus.)
despierta (v.)
día
disfrutar
distintos
dura
echa
empleados
entera
enviaré
escritor
eso
especial
espera (v.)
estrellas
evita
felices
fiesta
formar
fresca
fría
fruta
gente
hermana
hizo
hojas
horas
huevos
jamás
joven
jugando
labios
lado
le (pron.)
leen
levantar
llevan
lo (pron.)
luchan
manos
mantendrán
mayor
médicos
menores
menos
mensaje
mesa
mezclar
mil
modos (sus.)
negros
nieve
ninguno
no
noches
o (conj)
oscuro
oye
papel
parece
parte
pasa
pasó
pensó
personas
pesado
piel
pies
pintar
plan
plantas
platos
pocas
ponen
posible
prueba
puerta
rápidamente
rato
responder
rodea
rojo
rostro
saben
sale
seguro (adj.)
sentimientos
señora
si (conj.)
siete
siguiente
silencio
sirven
solito
sombra
suave
suele
sueño
suerte
tarde
temo
terrible
tipo
toca
toman
trabajar
una (nº)
usar
ven (venir)
ventanas
verano
vida
visiten
volver

DESTREZAS DE DESCODIFICACIÓN ENSEÑADAS HASTA LA FECHA

Palabras con *m;* palabras con *p;* palabras con *t;* palabras con *l;* palabras con *s;* palabras con *d;* palabras con *n;* palabras con *v;* palabras con *b;* palabras con *f;* palabras con *rr;* palabras con *r* y sílabas cerradas con *r; palabras con h;* palabras con *ge, gi, j;* palabras con *ca, co, cu, k, que, qui;* palabras con *y, ñ;* palabras con *ch;* palabras con *ll, w;* palabras con *cl;* palabras con *cr;* palabras con *ga, go, gu, gue, gui;* palabras con *ce, ci, za, zo, zu;* diptongos *ai, au, ay, ei, eu, ey, oi, oy;* diptongos *ia, ie, io, iu, ua, ue, ui, uy;* palabras con *tr;* diéresis: *güe, güi;* palabras con *bl;* palabras con *br;* palabras con *pl;* palabras con *pr;* palabras con *i, x* como *j;* palabras con *mb, mp;* palabras con *nn, nm;* palabras con *x,* la *x* como *j;* palabras con *cc, x.*